Remembering Happiness:

OCD & Depression

How to Battle Them and Finally Smile Again

By Charles K. St. Cross

Dedication

I dedicate this book to my dear family, my three angels who live and love a husband and father constantly struggling to be the best husband and father he can, despite his sickness. They are sent from God to get me through this life. They are my everything, the only reason I get up in the morning, all that matters, and my only sunshine in a world all too often shrouded in darkness. I love them with every fiber of my being. God bless them.

Table of Contents

Forward

A little-known fact is that Charles St. Cross was a teacher before he authored books.

....

"Oh my Gosh! Oh my Gosh! I got Mr. Hine for 4th grade next year," screamed Christian as he ran excitedly toward Mr. Hine's classroom!

It was the last day of school and students were receiving their report cards in which the name of their next year's teacher was written. Obviously, Christian's dream came true!

Charles became a popular teacher because of his ability to quickly build a learning community where students were appreciated, honored and inspired to do their 'personal best'. His passion for teaching was obvious!

It was a joy to watch Mr. St. Cross' interactions with his students and how he captured their attention. At the students' request, he even established extra enrichment literary groups that took place during recess and/or after school. Parents were delighted to give permission for their child to participate.

Charles was also a team player. The year before he was hired as a 4th grade teacher, he was our school intern. During that time, he was a substitute teacher, helped set up our new computer lab, enhanced his own technology skills, and evaluated educational software. He used these skills to support all of us in our new technology-training workshops.

He also volunteered to develop a spreadsheet-based method to help me manage our school's complex master schedule. This was a time-consuming, tedious project and Charles' solution was ingenious.

"Hey, is that Mr. St. Cross in the dunking booth? Let's try to dunk him…he would think that's funny!" It was our school's annual fundraising "Spring Fair" and students rushed to purchase balls to throw! By volunteering for 'hazardous duty' in the dunking booth, Charles helped raise money for our PTA. He also supported the PTA by attending evening meetings and giving input, when appropriate. His active involvement in the PTA helped him develop close ties with parents and, indirectly, with their children.

Mr. St. Cross left a successful accounting career to teach because he was looking for a more personally fulfilling career for him. Being older than the beginning teacher, he had a broader perspective and immediately observed that an exemplary school required teachers, staff and parents to work together as partners to create a school where children loved to learn and teachers loved to teach.

Therefore, he involved himself in all aspects of our school community. He was respected and liked by all who knew him…students, colleagues and parents. Mr. St. Cross was an exceptional teacher. I observed him in many different roles and he was superb in each. Indeed, Charles had it all!

Years later I discovered he performed his job while fighting his own private war with OCD and Depression. It was only at this time that he shared with me that while he carried on his work during the day, he would subsequently go home to his bed and cry for hours due to his conditions. A triumph in the eyes of his peers, students, and students' parents was personally picked apart by his obsessive disorder. While he succeeded in the view of everyone else, he believed himself to be an utter failure in his distorted mind.

It saddens me that he suffered so much, while adding such value to our school. I look very, very fondly on my years working with Charles and he has told me he feels the same. He continues to be a dear friend and I wish him well in his battle.

Dr. Patricia McIntosh Coles, Phd. Ed.

Preface

Alright, I'd like to get something straight right from the start. The reason I wrote this second book is trifold. I want to educate you about what you have. I want you to understand why you have the symptoms you do. Secondly, I'm not a doctor although I have three college degrees in other subject areas. But I am an expert in OCD and Depression for reasons that will soon be disclosed. I have had OCD and Depression for my entire life. And I've been around for about half a century. That's a lot of experience. I'll keep the chapters short if not few. Who wants long, drawn out chapters anyway? Besides, isn't it satisfying to think, "Hey I read a twenty-five-chapter book!" At the end of the book there will be two screening quizzes; one to see if you have OCD tendencies, and one to see if you show the characteristics of Depression. You may find them helpful if you are on the fence as to whether you should seek help in improving your psychological health.

Finally, and maybe *most importantly*, I want you to smile, snicker, and perhaps even laugh. I write this for a population of people who know suffering well and don't have much occasion for levity. If I can get you to laugh, I'll be very pleased. Sadness hurts, laughing heals. In that respect, I'm going to begin each chapter with a joke of some kind. You might even find them funny enough with which to chuckle along. I have a unique sense of humor, hopefully not so unique that I'm the only one who gets it. Enjoy!

A psychiatrist draws a picture of a house and shows it to his patient. He says, "What does this make you think of?"

The patient says, "Sex."

The doctor draws a second picture of a bicycle and shows it to his patient. He says, "What does this make you think of?"

The patient says, "Sex."

The psychiatrist draws a third picture, this time a car, and asks his patient, "What does this make you think of?"

The patient repeats, "Sex".

The doctor finally puts down his pencil and pad, sits back, and looks like his patient. He states, "You definitely have an obsession with sex.

*The patient immediately stands up and indignantly shouts, "**I** have an obsession with sex??? You're the one drawing all the dirty pictures!!!"*

Chapter 1: OC What?

Only the very special diseases, disorders and conditions get acronyms. OCD is one of them. Consider yourself privileged. You have a medical acronym. Congratulations! Diabetes can't say that. Multiple personalities can't either. You're special; so special you sometimes just don't even feel like going on. But seriously, Obsessive Compulsive Disorder is a vicious condition. It can steal your career, your friends, your loved ones, and even your life. This is my second book about OCD and Depression. And we'll talk later about why these two conditions are such comrades.

I've had OCD and Depression my whole life, 49 years. I wonder should I get to 50 if I'll get a pin or a watch from the National Institution of Mental Health. Doubt it. Yes, I'm 49 and have battled my whole life. If you question my street cred about these monsters, I can put your mind at ease. I have gone to no less than five psychiatrists, been on over 20 separate drugs in a plethora of combinations and dosages, have participated in individual and group therapy sessions galore, endured Cognitive Behavioral Therapy (CBT), survived Trans-Cranial Magnetic Stimulation Therapy (TMS), barely lived through Shock Therapy (ECT), traversed partial hospitalization programs, and been fully hospitalized at an Ivy League affiliated institution. So please hear this. My experiences cause my words to carry weight. Agree or disagree with me. But don't question my authority to speak on the subject. My life has been and still, to a degree, is dominated by these two disorders. If you want to learn to make a sweater, you listen to somebody who knits. Well I've got a truckload of God damned sweaters. Please listen to what I have to say. It's the real deal.

So, coming to the stark realization and disappointment that some of you have not read my first book, <u>I'm Not Sick, But I'm Not Well</u>, let's talk about what we're dealing with here. OCD or Obsessive-Compulsive Disorder carries the following definition: (We'll go to the International OCD Foundation website for this one.)

"Obsessive Compulsive Disorder (OCD) is a mental health disorder that affects people of all ages and walks of life and occurs when a person gets caught in a cycle of obsessions and compulsions. Obsessions are unwanted, intrusive thoughts, images or urges that trigger intensely distressing feelings. Compulsions are behaviors an individual engages in to attempt to get rid of the obsessions and/or decrease his or her distress.

Most people have obsessive thoughts and/or compulsive behaviors at some point in their lives, but that does not mean that we all have "some OCD." In order for a diagnosis of obsessive compulsive disorder to be made, this cycle of obsessions and compulsions becomes so extreme that it consumes a lot of time and gets in the way of important life activities that the person values." (7)

Ok, let's clarify a bit and try to put things in plain language.

You have an intrusive (disturbing, unsettling, unwanted) thought, mental image, or impulse. This is the **obsession (O).** Because of this you feel the need to do, say or think something to make it go away. You do this because you feel guilt for having the obsession. You know you can't make it go away, you've already had it, but you want to make it okay somehow. The feeling of needing to do, say, or think something to remedy the obsession is the **compulsion (C).** The actual following through with this act is termed a **ritual. (R)** So, while OCR makes more sense, OCD (D standing for disorder) is what all the medical textbooks say. So, we'll go with OCD to avoid a monumental recall. ☺

Now here's the me against OCD battle *strategy* in a nutshell. Huh, nutshell. I crack myself up. Every doctor you talk to will give you a similar, if not identical version of this. Ready? You have the intrusive thought or impulse; the obsession. You feel a strong need to do something to make it *right*; the compulsion. You do that something and your mind feels relieved and forgiven for the thought or impulse; the ritual. This is the typical cycle.

Now, how do you break the cycle? Here's the answer to all your problems! Write this down on your hand. DON'T DO NUMBER 3. Yup. That's it. It's what every therapist will tell you is the most direct route back to sanity. Just don't do the ritual. Why, because it's like a drug, an addictive drug. Doing it makes you feel better. But it's only temporary. It's your fix, but not a permanent one.

You see, it's the ritual that makes you different from the remainder of the human population. Everyone has obsessive thoughts. A common person may have a strong desire for their eating utensils to be in precise order; all in the correct compartment, facing the same way, stacked neatly. They actually think about it when they are, by chance, in the kitchen. They have the compulsion to scan the drawer every time they go to retrieve a fork or spoon. They are pleased when all utensils are in order and adjust them when they are not. But this is not a true ritual.

A ritual would be to deliberately go and look in the utensil drawer when you aren't in need of a fork or spoon, but solely to check for order; then straightening anything askew. A ritual causes you to alter your normal behavior in order to appease a compulsion. A person with severe OCD may check that same drawer several times a day for no other reason than to put their mind at ease by dismissing a distorted thought or fulfilling an inexplicable impulse.

This is a ritual and makes someone who is simply excessively meticulous into a person with OCD. It is a fine line, but a distinct one. This is just one example, as Obsessive Compulsive Disorder can take many other forms and manifest itself in a myriad of ways. And of course, doing the ritual makes it all that much easier to do the next time. Like I said, the ritual has addictive properties.

The Cycle That Needs to Be Broken

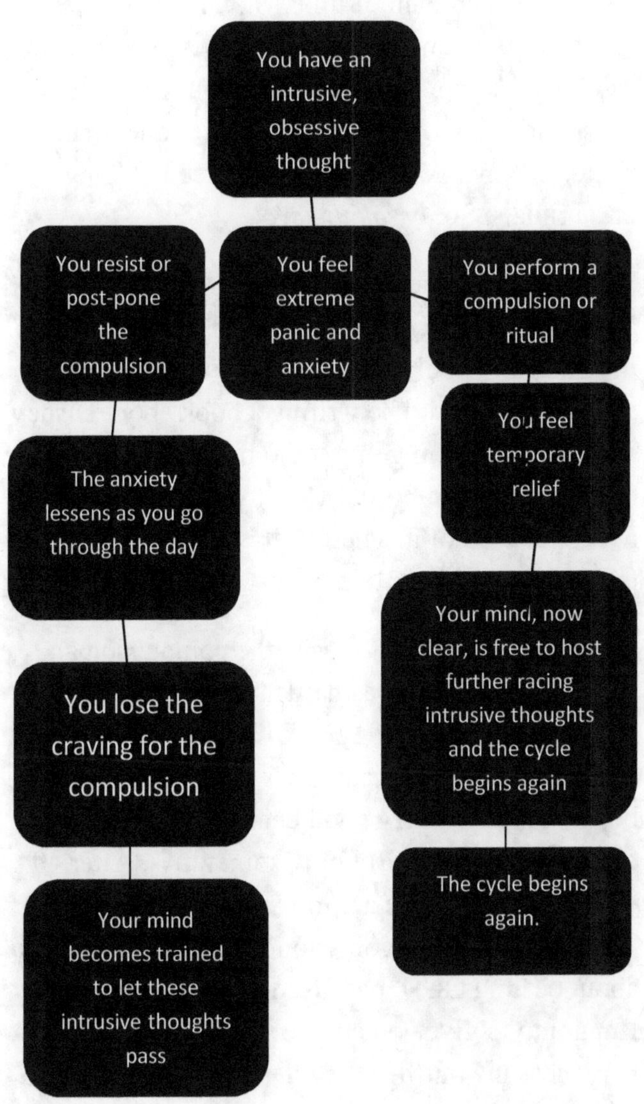

If you veer right on the diagram, you'll feel better for a limited amount of time. Now having a clear mind, you'll soon have another obsessive thought, and then a compulsion, and then you'll have to do the ritual again to feel better. Soon, sooner than you could imagine, your life is dominated by doing these rituals. So, *break the cycle.*

But if breaking the cycle was easy, no one would have OCD, drug companies would have little to do, psychiatrists would be spinning in their cool office chairs, and I would be writing a book about Disney World. Which I'm going to do because it's the happiest place on Earth. Don't you love Disney? I never get tired of it. There's always something new to do and the rides……..sorry, tangent there.

Anyway, it's HARD to resist the compulsion and not do the ritual; just as hard as it is for a drug addict to resist his next crack line. We're humans. If we are hurting, and we know what will make us feel better. There's a very good chance we're going to do it. I can resist it. But only sometimes. After 49 years of trying, there are too many times I give in. That's why I'm not going to lecture you in this book about beating OCD, because I can't always do it. I'm going to give you advice about finding happiness in your life *despite* this condition.

The receptionist of a psychiatrist knocks on the door of her employer, opens it a crack and whispers loud enough to hear, "Sir, there is a man outside who says he thinks he is invisible."

The doctor looks up from the papers on his desk and says, "I'm booked for today. Just tell him I can't see him."

Chapter 2: Where There's Smoke, There's Fire

OCD and Depression are a match made in heaven, or in this case hell. The agony of OCD often leads an individual toward the black hole of depression. (4) You could liken it to the chicken and the egg analogy, but when you think about it, OCD is really the chicken. Let's hit up the American Psychiatric Association for this one:

Depression is a common and serious medical illness that negatively affects how you feel, the way you think and how you act. Depression causes feelings of sadness and/or a loss of interest in activities once enjoyed. It can lead to a variety of emotional and physical problems, and can decrease a person's ability to function at work and at home. Depression symptoms can vary from mild to severe. (10)

I won't bore you with the long, long, list of symptoms someone with depression may feel. You know what it feels like to be depressed. I find it amusing how the experts state that the individual must exhibit the symptoms for *at least two weeks*. (2) So, if you are on day ten, you're still medically happy. (that's a scientific term) In four more days you can say you're officially depressed. 49 years slightly exceeds the fourteen-day benchmark, so I qualify for what they term major depression. (19) Don't be jealous. I'm *that* good.

The link between OCD and Depression is plain. By making every effort to break the cycle of Obsessive Compulsive Disorder, you are denying yourself something that will make you feel better. Until then you feel bad, and harbor that guilt for your unwanted thought, image, desire, or feeling. In this, you touch upon two big league symptoms of Depression; feeling sad in mood and feeling worthless or guilty. (1) Something that helps me to occupy my mind, not leave it open for undesired thoughts, and combats my feeling of worthlessness, is writing.

So, thank you for reading what I write, you're helping me as I hope to help you. You, in the same vein, should do something that occupies *your* mind and gives you a feeling of worth. Just make sure it's legal in your given state. Firework shows may occupy your mind, give you a sense of worth, and make you feel good, but it will also get you arrested in Connecticut. Jail time can be *really* depressing. I'm just sayin', word to the wise. 😉

Chapter 3: That Lucky Person

The truth is, you probably have a family and friends you rely on. You worry about them, and them about you. You need those family and friends. There is an old African proverb that says, "Many thin sticks, when bundled, are often unbreakable."

But combating OCD and Depression requires one SPECIAL person. The first and best thing to do for yourself if you suffer from OCD, Depression, or both is to find that special person that can serve as your safety net. Despite the best medications and management strategies, there will be times when you lose the battle.

The famed 1927 Yankees lost 44 times. Even if you are on the right medications and are using the right self-help strategies and techniques, there will be times when you are outmatched. Even after a half century of combating these conditions, there are days I don't want to go on; times when I cry face down in my pillow in bed; neutral as to whether I care to wake up or not.

It is that time that my wife steps in and just comforts me, assuring me that whatever is bothering me will pass. Letting me know that she won't leave my side as I face my demons. You need that person...because the pain you feel is **real**. No one else may believe you, but I DO. And it's at those times that real sufferers consider doing bad things to themselves.

Educate yourself about your conditions. Know thy enemy and know them well. You have to understand that you feel the pain that you feel because you have a chemical imbalance in your brain. (3) It's not something you can help. Your thoughts and feelings are tainted because of a skewed mind. Your perception of reality is distorted. The pain not only emanates from your thoughts and feelings. Most of the hurt comes from the guilt you bear because of them.

You wouldn't feel guilty about having cystic fibrosis. It is a horrible disease that you combat as best you can, given the drugs and life management techniques you've been taught and have learned. For some reason though, because OCD and Depression are psychologically based, with symptoms that manifest themselves in the mind, we think we should be able to control them; that we can *will* the illness away. We lose site of the painful truth of these medical conditions easily. It is *then* that we most desperately need that lucky person. One that knows the truth, can remind us of it, and can talk us back off the proverbial, yet all too real, ledge.

My mother was that person growing up. She knew nothing of the chemistry going on in my brain. She just knew she loved me and showed her sympathy for my pain at every turn. My wife has stepped in for her now and she has an in-depth knowledge of the causes and manifestations of OCD and Depression. God has blessed me with her. She recognizes my symptoms as they occur each day and gives me the support I need to win that day's battle.

Pick your person carefully, as they can push you off that ledge as easily as reel you back in. My father knew nothing of the conditions of Depression and OCD. His response to my behavior was to "straighten up" and "stop with the stupid thoughts." He was a Marine and had no tolerance for what he considered imaginary problems or the "shrinks" that dealt with them. He made that clear to me and drove me deeper into my teenage abyss. Then he just distanced himself from me. Keep what you don't understand at arm's length right?

He became less and less a part of my world, and in this, possibly saved my life. I loved him and I am sure he loved me. But he had no frame of reference to deal with a son with psychological problems. In my heart, I know he would do something to help me if he could. He simply didn't have the tools. *Find* someone who is willing to acquire the tools. It may save your life.

Chapter 4: Where Are My Damned Glasses???

This is something I probably say to myself at least three times a day. I wear glasses for distance even though I had LASIK surgery in the year 2000. I guess over the past two decades my eyes have deteriorated to the point where glasses are a necessity again. Anywho, every time I utter that curse, it reminds me of something my first psychiatrist told me when I was a young man.

This doctor was very old and a straight shooter. He was crippled in one leg and considering the width of his glasses, virtually blind. Still, he was like a grandpa with a lot of experience and horse sense. Despite this, much of the education he gave me came in parables. Jesus often taught in parables, so it's been validated by someone who is quite well known.

I was young and at that point knew practically nothing about the causes of OCD or Depression. I came to him thinking he would give me some secret to beat the disorder or jot a prescription that would erase my troubles.

Instead, one of the wisest things he told me was this: "Charles, you're like a confused, eccentric, old man I used to know. You see, this man lost his glasses in the parlor one day. So, each succeeding day, he would look for them outside under the street lamp. One day a neighbor got the courage to ask him, "Sir, you told me you lost your glasses in the house. Why do you keep looking for them outside under the streetlamp?" The old man said, "Because the light is better here!"

My doctor told me this purposefully. He wished to to draw an analogy. I was looking for the cures to my ailments through a quick bit of advice or a pill. He was trying to tell me that the answer to combating my conditions had to come from within. I could be assisted through medications or quick advice, but I had to win the internal fight to make any progress. He said, and this is how he expressed himself, that I should tell myself that there was no time to be crazy. I had a wife and kid and they needed a sound-minded husband and father. And you know what? Sometimes that reasoning actually worked. Sometimes it still does.

That doctor has long since retired due to his health, but his wisdom had more than some merit, and I think the profession would benefit from a little more of his perspective on things. I wish him happiness in the time he has left. We would do well to follow his advice.

We might also be shrewd to try what the doctor told Bob to do in the movie <u>What About Bob?</u> This is a great movie with a funny, quirky, multi-phobic character in it whom only Bill Murray could play. But his doctor's "prescription" to him was to "take a vacation; a vacation from your problems."

This, although from a comedic setting, is not comedic advice if you can do it. Take a day, a week, a month, whatever, and make the effort (I know this is hard and sometimes impossible) and ignore what's bothering you internally for a specific, distinct, predetermined time period. It's the knowledge that there's a distinct time period that makes it work. You'll take solace in that you'll eventually perform the ritual. Just not now. And after that time period, hopefully you've even forgotten your worry and will have beaten the cycle. Baby steps. See the movie. In the main character, you'll see a part of yourself.

In one way or another, we're all confined by invisible fencing.

Chapter 5: Good Morning...No, Not at All!

Now, by far, the most difficult part of the day is the morning. You see my midday medication is taken before the morning medication wears off. The nighttime medication is taken before bed and helps me through the night. But by morning, the effectiveness of any medications I've taken the previous day is no more. Yes, I know some medications stay in your system if you take them on a regular basis, but Vyvance (my anti-anxiety medication) and Clonipin (my sedative) are largely not those types. (11) So, after eight hours when I wake up, I immediately spiral out of control. It takes a while for my meds to kick in, and "the while" is hell.

My wife used to tell me to lie down, but I know that is the worst thing I could do. Lying on a bed thinking is not the best setting for an OCD patient. I get up almost crying, shaking and mumbling how

I'll *never* make it through the day. I make coffee and chug it down like I'm Moses and have been wandering the desert for 40 years. Then I try to find something in my house to occupy my mind like read or go through mail. I open all the shades and try to drink in the sunshine. Oddly enough, when I stare into the sun (don't try this at home) and the light hits the back of my eyes, I feel a little bit better. Kudos to Sting and his song Lithium Sunset. It seems to work. You see the Sun gives off lithium and……. nevermind, but listen to the song. It's about OCD, poignant, and heartbreaking.

I can't describe the panic and depression I feel before the medications begin to help. At that time, I don't have my safety net. My wife is getting our kids ready for school and getting ready for work herself. She has no time to comfort me and hold my hand through the agony. I understand this. Some people say they hate mornings. They have *no* idea. The day passes; sometimes well and sometimes torturously.

Then the meds kick in. I could feel it. By 9:00 a.m. to 9:30 a.m., I feel a little calmer. I feel I can accomplish something that day. I'm going to bed now knowing I will wake up in hell. It's an awful feeling; one that I get every night. Yes, sometimes I waver as to whether I want to wake up or not. Very sad, but I swear it's true.

If you are obsessive-compulsive, then keep checking that you pressed the right number.
If you are co-dependent, please ask someone to press 2.
If you have multiple personalities, please press 3, 4, 5, and 6.
If you are paranoid-delusional, we know who you are and what you want. Just stay on the line so we can trace the call.
If you are schizophrenic, listen carefully and a little voice will tell you which number to press.
If you are depressed, it doesn't matter which number you press. No one will answer.

Chapter 6: Check Please!...and One More Time

One trait that people with OCD often share is the habit of checking things. (15) It usually takes me a full 8-10 minutes to leave the house. First, I have to check the backdoor and make sure it is locked. Next, I need to check the stove to make sure all of the burners are off. Then I need to check the upstairs to make sure all the lights are off. Then I need to make sure the television is off. Next, I need to make sure the refrigerator and freezer are closed. Then I need to make sure the front door is locked. Next, I need to make sure the cat's door is open so he can access the litter box. After that I need to make sure the fireplace is closed, although there is no fire. Then I need to make sure the strip of wood we use to buttress the back-patio slider door is in place. Then I can leave the house and enter the garage, while pushing on the door to make sure it latched. Finally, I can get in my car, open the garage door, and *quickly* pull out. It seems like a simple walk through but it's not what it seems. It's hellish.

You see, I don't just look at the stove knobs to make sure they're off. I need to stare at each one for three full seconds. Then I need to do each one again until I've done each of them four times. I need to pull the door at least twice. I need to stare at the closed door for the total duration of my walking down the stairs. I literally can go on and on, but I trust you get the idea. It is bizarre I know…and agonizing.

I read once that some doctors call this a patient's doubting mechanism. I know something to be true, but then doubt my conviction. I know there is no fire in the fireplace, we haven't had a fire in three days. *But, what if there is?* Somehow, what if one of the embers survived. So, I check the door and know that it's closed. But as I walk away, I think, *what if it's not?* What if I didn't pull the handle properly and it's not closed? So, I turn around and go and do it again. I kid you not. I have driven halfway down the street and turned around to make sure the garage doors are closed even though I closed them and stared at them for the obligatory three seconds before I pulled away. Please don't laugh. It hurts.

When I was in college I lived upstairs at my parent's house and would walk up and down the stairs up to 15 times doubting that I sufficiently made sure the closet light was off. Why? FEAR! If I left the light on it could burst and start a fire and burn the house down and it would be MY fault. Why do I pull out of the garage quickly? Because what if the exhaust from the car blows into the garage, seeps through the walls, enters the house and harms my family? If you don't have OCD, you have NO idea of the anxiety. All this to go to the corner store and get a gallon of God damned milk. What a common person does mindlessly cripples a sufferer of OCD. I don't expect healthy people to understand. Just try to sympathize a little.

*I have had a multiple personality disorder in the
past, but we're all feeling better now.*

Chapter 7: I'll Trade You OCD for Diabetes…
and I'll Throw in Multiphobic Disorder

One of the worst things about having a
psychological disorder is the stigma attached to it.
(5) You would never call in to work and say you
couldn't come in that day because you were
depressed. You'd probably be fired. People with
psychological conditions are discriminated against.
A secretary could be allowed certain freedoms
because she has carpal tunnel. But she would never
be given any allowances if she told her boss she was
having a OCD episode.

Yes, I'm going to say it. I'm going on record right
here and now. Yes, I would much rather have
diabetes, migraines, an ulcer, autism, ADHD,
arthritis, severe food allergies, anorexia, or gout as
opposed to OCD and Depression. Some people say
this statement minimizes these afflictions. I don't
care! At least there is somewhat of a public
understanding and real sympathy for these
conditions. In large part, people have no idea of the
pain sufferers of OCD and Depression endure *every
day*.

People have a bad day and say, "Nothing is going
right for me today. Everything I do turns out wrong!
I'm so depressed." Or, for instance, they glibly
claim, "I had to count the change twice. Must be my

OCD!" They throw the terms around lightly and carelessly. You would *never ever* hear someone say, "I'm so out of breath today, I'm probably developing cystic fibrosis." It would justly be considered horrible to say something like that! Yet people can acceptably be flippant with OCD and Depression, the terms of conditions that completely steal people's happiness, ruin their very lives, and sometimes drive them to suicide! They should be ashamed.

When someone who has one of the conditions mentioned above, people acknowledge their plight and they are woefully pitied. They are showered with sympathy. Modifications and allowances are made to help them deal with the hand they were dealt.

Few, if not less, people even truly know the true nature of OCD. The average person just thinks you're one of those comic individuals who washes their hands 25 times a day. I don't wash my hands 25 times a day! (it's more like 15) But seriously, they have no idea of the multitude of symptoms and the pain they inflict on an OCD sufferer.

Depression is worse. Most people honestly just can't see why we don't just cheer up. They think, "Stop letting things bother you!" They think, "What are you worrying about anyway." They think, "You're just being a baby, toughen up". They have no idea that our lack of happiness goes much deeper than imaginable. They've never felt what it's like being in that endless black hole that seems inescapable. How inescapable? Enough to make some poor souls want to end their life to find peace. (6)

When I was at my worst, my wife would leave for work and I would lie in bed and cry all day. I would think of the easiest way to end my life if I were to actually consider it. It would have to be something that was quick and minimally painful. I would go to my bag of medication and count the Klonapin to guess if there was enough to kill me if I took them all. I then considered the worry that I would accidentally live through the suicide attempt and they would keep me in a psychiatric hospital for years.

Being in a mental institution for any period of time is beyond horror. There are dangerous people there. I've come face to face with them. I spoke with someone in the psychiatric ward who told me he took twenty Klonipin and lived through it. But the bottom line is that I could never leave my family no matter how horrific the constant pain. I don't know what lays ahead for me in the afterlife. I know I have three angels here; my wife and my two sons. An angel in the hand is worth….wait that's about birds. You have to laugh or all you'd do is cry.

Yes, I'd trade diseases or disorders with many people. I'm not afraid to say it and I won't apologize for it. Do your worst. What is worse, dying or living every day wanting to die? I don't know. I used to pray for hours for God to take me in my sleep. I just wanted the pain to end somehow. What can top praying to die so you can finally be at peace? Not much. Let's move on to lighter fare and maybe enjoy a chuckle together.

Checklist Nightmare for OCD Patients

☑ **Closet Color Coordinated**
☑ **Food Closet Alphabetize**
☑ **Laces Same Length**
☐ **Last Box Left Unchecked**

Chapter 8: Counting Onions… and Other Important Things I Do

Ok, this may be productive for you. As a lifetime member of the OCDUC (uk-duk) or Obsessive Compulsive Disorder Unofficial Club, I can share many of the symptoms I suffer from so you don't think you're weird, or God forbid, normal. Normal people are so *common*.

As you read previously, I check things. Check, check, check, check, check. That, we've covered. I also order things. If the candles are not lined up on the table I fix them. It bothers me. If the shoes on the floor are not even and on the proper side to put them on, I rearrange them. If there are dishes scattered in the sink I put them in the dishwasher. That's normal right? No, they have to be placed in the dishwasher from small plate to big going from left to right. Pictures. Why do we have to have so many damned pictures? They're never straight. I straighten them. Who could live with a crooked picture?

Chairs are an issue. If no one is sitting in them, they should be pushed in; all of them, always. In fact, it bothers me when someone is sitting in a chair askew to the table. It bothers me a lot. But what am I going to do? Tell them to get up and straighten their chair? They might think I have OCD and we've talked about the stigma that's attached to that. Drawers that aren't pushed in should be illegal. Someone could walk right into one of those. You should always park *straight* in the driveway. The driveway was paved straight for a reason, right? Vacuuming is never fun. Did I get the spots behind the doors? Did I get far enough under the bed? You've got to get everywhere. Have you ever heard of dust allergies? I don't want anyone developing those on my watch.

We talked about getting out of the garage as quickly as possible after starting the car. We're talking poisonous gases here. We're on the road now but we can't pull away, and for good reason ;-) We have to watch the garage doors close all the way. They have those invisible beams that cause the doors to retract if something breaks the beam. I've seen this happen when the wind blew a leaf in the track of one of those beams. The door went right back up. 99.99% of the time this doesn't happen. You know what that means? It means *there's a chance!*

Now at the store, other quirks, or some might more accurately say "tortures", come into play. The biggest challenge is getting the latest expiration date for everything. Yes, I know if the eggs say they're good for three week you're good. But if you get the eggs that are good for three weeks and two days…they're *FRESHER*! Sure, I look odd with eight dozen eggs under my left arm as I reach to the very back of the shelf with the right. I haven't dropped………many. People look at me funny, but they'd understand if they knew I had OCD. In lieu of that they probably think I'm the weird, peculiar, potentially disturbed guy who shops at their store. Hmmm….I can live with that for FRESHER eggs!

I also check every can I buy for dents through the same procedure. The irony is that I create more dents in cans by dropping them than there was in the first place. Oh well, that's the next person's problem. *I* …..have perfect cans, and that's all that matters. And yes, finally, I count the onions so I get the bag with the most.

Well that's just a taste of my eccentric mannerisms as an OCD sufferer. And if you do some of these things, you're not alone. It's part of your condition. (9) And, all humor aside, having to do these rituals is extraordinarily painful and acutely stressful. We'll talk about some things you can do to combat them soon. But at least knowing you're not alone in performing these bizarre formalities of normal life functions is a start.

Two elderly couples were enjoying friendly conversation when Charlie asked the other, "Fred, how was the memory clinic you went to last month?"

"Outstanding," Fred replied. "They gave me some great memory strategies."

Charlie says, "That's great! What was the name of the clinic?"

Fred went blank. He thought and thought but admitted he just couldn't remember. Fred says to Charlie, "In the past I'd be stumped, but instead I'm going to use a strategy."

Fred asked Charlie, "What do you call that red flower with the long stem and thorns?" Charlie answers, "You mean a rose?"

Fred exclaims, "Yes, that's it!" He turns to his wife next to him and asks. . ."Hey Rose, what was the name of that clinic?"

Chapter 9: Is There a Doctor in the House? A Good One?

There are many doctors out there. Some are great and some are just awful. I'm lucky right now to be with one of the excellent doctors in the profession. He has respect for my intelligence, my knowledge of these conditions, my understanding of applicable medications, the places I've been, the programs I've

attended, my vast experience, the long road I've
traveled, and places trust in what I feel I need in
terms of my care. I, in turn, have tremendous
respect for his intelligence, great expertise, trust,
and compassion. I can't say much more due to
doctor/patient confidentiality. You understand.

What I'd like to talk to you about right now is about
that very first doctor I had many years ago and
discussed earlier. Why? Because he was a good
doctor, but also a really entertaining character. As
you know he was very elderly and spoke with what
I can best describe as an elderly Italian/Jewish
accent. Think Jackie Mason mixed with Mario from
Nintendo.

When I showed up for an appointment he would
say, with feigned surprise, "You're back, I guess I
didn't succeed in scaring you off." He would start
each session with his definition of OCD. After a
year it was rote memory for me. In fact, I've told
you he was virtually blind. For this reason, I think,
he rarely looked at me. He would recline in his
chair and stare into space. Knowing he was not
paying any attention to me, I would mouth the
definition, just to test myself. I knew it by heart.

He was one of those psychiatrists who knew a lot;
he had many, many years of experience and had
seen the evolution of the profession itself, and
sometimes liked to show it. There were many times
he would lecture me about the existence, absence,
interaction, or overactivity of the chemicals in my

brain, which was fascinating. He was a brilliant man, this I give him. He took no notes but seemed to remember everything. But there were also times when he would talk about how I reminded him of his son and how that caused him to have a greater affinity for me than most other patients.

He would, at times, go off on some tangent about something or other and I would begin to look distracted. That's when his character would often appear. I would get (remember to read this with the described accent), "What? I'm talking here and I'm doubting about the listening! I'm old, but I know when the hearing thing is not followed by the listening. What do you say we do a little focusing? I don't know how much time I have left ya know. I might say something important." He said this all tongue in cheek and it was hilarious to me. He made me laugh when I had forgotten how. I appreciated this. So much so I'm sharing his tales in two chapters.

Once I told him about how I always feel very subconscious and as though everyone's looking at me when I walk in a room and noticing all the things that are wrong with my appearance. He would retort "Kid," he always called me kid, "you've got typical dysmorphophobia or what is known as body dysmorphic disorder." Then he would go on to say, "But I'm telling you kid, you have no right to have this particular phobia. You're a good-looking kid. People should all want to look as good as you! I'm just sayin', hey you're no

Fernando Llamas but you're still pretty handsome. Lorenzo Llamas maybe, but not Fernando. Worry about how *they* look, not you. You're fine. Would I lie about something as crucial as superficial, cosmetic appearance? Probably not. Take solace in that."

Anyway, this is a thumbnail sketch of my very first psychiatrist. He taught me a lot when I was on a very steep learning curve. My conditions also weren't nearly as severe then and his antics often lifted my spirits. As I said, he is in his 80's now and retired. He is crippled in one leg and can't see the hand in front of his face. He's sold his estate and now lives with his wife, who dutifully cares for him, in a condo locally.

I truly wish he was in better health and could better enjoy his retirement. I reached out to him recently and he said "How did you find me. I'm in the Psychiatrist Witness Protection Program. They must be slackin' off." We chatted about the old times and he assured me (wink, wink) that if I begged him he'd even consider taking me back. He *always* made me laugh, like I'm trying to make you laugh a little. Pay it forward right? I wish him well.

The nurse asked, "So how's your breakfast this morning?" The old woman replied "It's very good, except for the Kentucky Jelly. I can't seem to get used to the taste."

The confused nurse asked, "Kentucky jelly? What makes you think the jelly is from Kentucky?"

The elderly patient replied, "It says it right on the package", and produced a foil packet stating "KY Jelly".

Chapter 10: Swallowing Fourteen Pills at Once is Not a Marketable Skill
(your resume will not benefit)

I can't promise you any laughs in this chapter. This is all about the business of drugs; drugs to help you get by. For years, when I was first diagnosed with OCD and Depression, Prozac (used to treat major depressive disorder, obsessive-compulsive disorder, and panic disorder) helped me a great deal. Then suddenly as I grew older, it just stopped having any benefit. At that point I took a DNA test to show which psychological drugs might have the greatest chance to help me. Sit down. Listen to this. The test came back stating that in my current state it was unlikely that any more than 5% of psychological drugs would aid my condition. I was crushed.

Since then I've tried drug after drug looking for the five needles in a haystack that would help me in my struggle. My current doctor is superb and has tried many variations of medications on me. He prescribes, I give feedback, and he makes adjustments as to drug or dose. He has me moving in the right direction. He knows I have a ways to go before I lead a normal life. But his knowledge and patience have given me hope.

I'm sure you are wondering exactly what I take, especially if you are a sufferer and are taking a cocktail of medications that are not working. Let me share with you. I take:

Vyvance, which is actually for ADHD in older children and adults, and for severe B.E.D. (binge eating disorder) in adults. It curbs my anxiety considerably.

Klonopin (or Clonazepam) is used in the treatment of Panic Disorder (this, I need) and in the treatment of certain convulsive seizure disorders, such as (would you believe) epilepsy. It affects chemicals in the brain that may be unbalanced. (such as mine)

Keppra is another anti-epileptic drug, and also called an anticonvulsant. It's used as adjunctive therapy to treat partial onset seizures in adults with epilepsy.

Remeron is used to treat Depression. It improves mood and feelings of well-being. (a must for me) It's an antidepressant that works by restoring the balance of natural chemicals (neurotransmitters) in the brain.

Pristiq is an antidepressant belonging to a group of drugs called selective serotonin and norepinephrine reuptake inhibitors (SNRIs). It affects chemicals in the brain that may be unbalanced in people with major Depressive Disorder. (like me)

Zyprexa is used to treat certain mental/mood conditions such as Schizophrenia and Bipolar Disorder. It may also be used in combination with other medication to treat Depression. It's considered an atypical antipsychotic.

Synthroid is a prescription medication that can help treat hypothyroidism. Synthroid can help restore thyroid hormone balance. It is a man-made thyroid hormone identical to thyroxine, the hormone that's naturally made by the thyroid gland.

NAC is a supplement. And, as supplements go, one that might be among the most important ones you could take. NAC has broad benefits to health. Because it contains both sulfur and the amino acid cysteine, NAC serves as a precursor to glutathione-a key antioxidant that provides protection against free radicals and toxins in the body.

Niacin is a supplement for metabolism and energy. All B vitamins help the body convert food (carbohydrates) into fuel (glucose), which the body uses to produce energy.

Choleast or Red Yeast Rice is for cholesterol (nuf said) No wait, it also helps maintain healthy lipid particle size and number. (I'm always concerned about my lipid particle size. Number? Not so much.)

Vitamin B-Referred to as vitamin B complex, (because it sounds cooler) are the eight B vitamins — B1, B2, B3, B5, B6, B7, B9, B12 — that play an important role in converting our food into fuel, allowing us to stay energized throughout the day.

Vitamin D is for bones and immunity. You need it to absorb calcium and promote bone growth. You also need vitamin D for other important body functions. (of which I do not know, but have not been proven through clinical trials, so it doesn't matter) But, it has been linked, if only loosely, to depression. (Plus, it's cheap, so why the hell not.)

Multivitamins are used to provide vitamins that are not taken in through the diet. Who doesn't take a multivitamin? I mean….come on! But, they always say in bold print, **Never take more than the recommended dose.** I find this funny because I never heard of anyone losing the will to live and deciding to commit suicide by taking a handful of multivitamins. And you know what? I personally have taken more than the recommended dose, and I'm still here. Yes, I've taken up to four multivitamins, all at once! Yes, I'm a rebel; dangerous even. (11)

Well, anyway this is what I like to call my current cocktail of medications. So far, they have given me fairly good support to use my management techniques and strategies in an effort to have relatively normal days. If you didn't notice, relatively is underlined. Keyword, if there ever was one. Normal people have normal days. I can have a day or two, here and there, where I can find some proximity to normal. For now, that's what I shoot for. I'm a realist. Rome wasn't built in a day. (Why is the saying always about Rome? Was it somehow especially hard to build? What did the Romans say? "Egypt wasn't built in a day ya know!" Why don't we say that instead? I mean they had the Pyramids, the Sphinx…..and all in the heat of the desert. I know it was a dry heat, but still! God knows that couldn't have been easy.)

Sorry. I'm OCD. I constantly have racing thoughts. Often not rational. I can't always control it. Forget what I said. We'll stick with Rome. Everybody's used to it. Nobody likes change, except maybe the Romans. I hear they kept building for years.

There is no joke for this next chapter because there is a major part of my life that is no joke.

Chapter 11: God Help Me

I'm writing this chapter because you need to know how I really am. I almost always write when I'm having a good day; when I have the motivation. But today I am going to show you the other side of my life. I woke up in a panic. I dreamt all night. I know I had bad thoughts but I can't remember them. I don't want to remember them. But I feel horrible. I feel *tremendously* guilty. I feel shaky, anxious, panicked, worried. I wish I went to sleep and didn't wake up. I would finally have sanctuary in heaven.

I don't know what I'm worried about. I got up and my wife told me I had to go and get a few groceries today and then go to the pet store for food. I can't do that! I don't want to leave the house today! I can't! What if I make a mistake? What if I make a mistake because of a stray, unwanted thought? I won't be able to forgive myself. And I won't be able to talk to my wife. She'll be at work and can't take calls. I don't want to get up. I just want to stay here under the covers where it is safe. I can't go out there and see people. What if they ask me a question? What if I see someone I know and they see me in this condition? What will I say? I'm gonna make a mistake I just know it. Oh God here I go.

(I get up and start the day)

I knew it. I blew it. I was doing ok, I hadn't made any mistakes. But then it happened. Because my mind was distracted by an unwanted thought I drove right past the pet store. I panicked and crossed over into the oncoming lane and swerved into a vacant lot. There was snow there and it scraped the bottom of my car? What if the car is damaged; all because of me? Why? Why did I do it? I'm worthless. I can't do anything right! I am flustered. I turn around and merge into traffic. A car beeps at me. That bastard! Doesn't he know how I feel dammit! I go back to the pet store. I buy the food. As I am leaving the store and I realize I didn't get the big size like my wife told me to. DAMMIT! Now I'm spiraling down and down; feeling worse; and worse; and mistakes are turning into more mistakes. I have to go in, return the medium bag and buy the large one. I want to go home and just cry. But I have to go to the supermarket.

My OCD is peaking now. I find myself standing at the banana stand comparing the lengths of the bananas, making sure to get the longest ones. I have to. I pick a bunch, but one has a brown mark on it. Should I still get it? I don't know. I throw them in the cart. I have to not cry! I need bread. I pull the whole shelf of bread out and compare the dates. I find one with the latest date and inspect it for imperfections. I can't find any. Bread, check. Bacon is next. I go through every one looking for the latest date. But then I have to compare them for the amount of fat I see. There must be 20 to examine. I take the package, after going through every one, that I deem the leanest. I need cooking spray. I pick up each bottle to see which one feels heaviest. That means it has more in it, right. I take what I feel is the heaviest one. Lastly, I go to get cereal. All the boxes are identical. I take the third one from the front. The third; three, because I have three angels in my life; my wife and my two sons. Whenever all things are equal I go with the number three.

This is just my morning. But I get to go home now; a preserve from the outside world. I need to do things that will take my mind off the horrible mistakes I've made. I vacuum, making sure that I get every spot in the house; under couches and beds included. I do the rugs. I do the one in our bedroom and as I'm leaving the room I get this feeling that I rushed, so I go back and do it again. It takes me an hour and forty-five minutes to do a 2000 square foot house. My wife takes about forty-five minutes. I go on to empty the dishwasher, inspecting every piece as I take it out. Most make the cut, but there are always three or four that I don't consider clean *enough* and I put them back in.

I've got to go pick up my son from school soon. This is the most important thing I'll do all day. I have to get there and get a spot where he can just walk right out of school and into the car. I set alarms in the house to alert me that it's almost time to go. I arrive 30 minutes before the end of school. No one is there. Why would there be, thirty minutes before school even ends. I'm assured of my spot. I sit there and look at the trees as I wait for the bell. Joseph, my son, comes out and jumps right into the car. Mission accomplished.

OK…I could painfully go on. But I promised you I would be honest in my writing. My life is not humorous or amusingly sarcastic. It is pain. These are my conditions in action and you need to know that I have more than my share of these types of days.

My writing is my heartfelt attempt to share information about our conditions and make you smile or even laugh. But the real life I lead is *this* chapter.

Yes, God help me…please.

*Doctor: Ma'am, exactly how long have you believed
you are a cat?*

Patient: Oh God, since I was just a kitten.

Chapter 12: Parental Guidance

It has been concluded in some studies that OCD and
Depression may be linked to DNA. (8) This means
that some people who have a history of OCD and
Depression may be predisposed to having these
conditions. There is no way to tell for sure, but the
empirical evidence supports the theory. (13) If I
was part of this research, they would definitely
conclude that these conditions run within our
deoxyribonucleic acid, which carries our genetic
instructions, so to speak.

It is known, but never spoken of, that my great
grandfather on my father's side was prone to
massive mood swings and violence. He was a
strong man but ended his own life with a shotgun in
the family barn. I don't judge people who die by
their own hand. Not everyone has a loving family
to live for. You don't know how painful
psychological conditions can be. Not everyone can
fight the demons indefinitely. Some are brave
enough to escape in other ways. Yes, I just said that.
On my worst days I admire the poor souls like
Robin Williams who end their suffering on their
own terms.

The people who suffer from their internal demons
and don't have any special someone to continue to
live for are (and I truly believe this) courageous. It
can't be easy to take your own life. These people
do it because they lost the battle and are just looking
for peace. How can you blame someone who lives
with constant pain and anguish for seeking final
peace? I can't. I've told you, I've had thoughts of
suicide, but I could never do it. I have three angels
in my life that I'd never abandon. Ever.

My grandfather on my mother's side had the same
mood swings. He was in the Italian mafia and
would be prone to fits of verbal and physical abuse.
He would regularly hit my grandmother, who
dutifully took it. One time, just one time, my mother
stood up and said, "Daddy please stop!" That
afternoon my grandfather took my mother's *four*
toys and burned them in the backyard while making
her watch. Tell me that guy didn't have some
psychological problems going on! I never knew
him. He died way before I came around. Don't
know that I missed much.

But I'm not here to give you a complete family
history. I want to focus on my mother and father.
Neither my mother nor my father made it past their
freshman year in high school. My father had very
limited intelligence and school was incredibly hard
for him. Back in the day, he was the feature of an
article in a prominent magazine discussing the fate
of boys who were of very little intellect. Can you
believe it? They wrote an article to highlight a

young man whom they termed "stupid". This was
the very late 1940's. When one of the interviewers
spoke with his mother (my grandmother), she said
"They should probably let Artie just drop out and
give the desk to someone who could think better."
She said this! His own mother. Is it a wonder he
dropped out soon thereafter and joined the Marines?

Dad found self-confidence and pride in the Marines.
He and my mother were beautiful people. They had
honest to goodness movie star looks. Think James
Dean and a prettier Dorothy Lamour. People would
call them this on the street. They were knockouts.
That's why *I* am so….nope, not gonna say it. Once
when Dad was in full official Marine garb, a general
came up to him and said, "Young man, you look
like a real Marine. How would you like to go to
Paris and stand guard outside the office of our
ambassador to France?" This was the time of the
Korean War and would mean he wouldn't go to
Korea into battle, but instead to a cushy office in
Paris.

He responded, "Thank you sir, but with all due
respect, I want to fight like my brothers." (They
were in the Navy and Army.) He could have
avoided the war altogether, but passed it up. So, he
went to battle and nearly got his leg blown off by a
mortar shell. He subsequently received the Purple
Heart and was on the list to head home. Instead, he
requested to be sent back to the front lines. This is
an example of why the men and women of this time
are called the Greatest Generation. I could go on

with this topic. But I won't. I just want to say, although my Dad was not the finest father in the world, I'll always have the utmost respect for him due to what he did for our country. Sempre Fi Dad. (Latin for "Always Faithful"…and with what every good Marine greets each other)

What is also important here is that Dad always showed signs of Depression and OCD. He would get up at around 4:30 am. (I don't ever remember getting up at 4:30 a.m. I'm not even sure 4:30 a.m. exists. I'll have to research that one.) and cut his nails until they bled. He would take no part in making decisions about buying cars, furniture, kitchen appliances, or any other significant item because he was afraid he'd give bad advice. These are all signs of my conditions, and that was just the tip of the iceberg.

He would stare at the television, and when you asked him what he was watching, he'd have no idea at all. He was just in his own mind thinking things over and over. He wouldn't go to the neighborhood hardware store unless he was wearing good clothes because someone might see him. He would make me show up to my little league games an hour and a half ahead of time because he was afraid we'd be late. He'd sit in his lawn chair with me on the grass next to him. (An hour and a half sitting at an empty field.) You can't play catch with yourself and he wasn't moving from that damned lawn chair.

In my unprofessional, yet educated decision, Dad had OCD and some degree of Depression. Despite this, he went to work every day in a 100-degree factory and welded hot metal to put food on the table. That cannot be ignored and must be respected.

Now my mother never saw a psychologist or psychiatrist, but even an educated layman such as I can tell you she also suffered greatly from OCD and Depression. Before I met Sofia, my beautiful wife and angel, my mother was the love of my life. She sacrificed in every possible way for me, my brother, and my sister. She also just plain showed the most love for us. When I was child I worshiped my mother. As Dad withdrew from making any decisions, Mom really became the head of the household.

Dad grew up in a cold household and I believe he didn't know how to show he cared. My mother showered us with love; tangible and intangible. She would play with us, watch television with us, cook for us, sleep with us when we were sick, clean up when we *got* sick, complimented us, helped us with schoolwork (I don't think dad attended even one of my parent teacher conferences), supported us, and shopped for our clothes… just to begin. We loved Dad, but we had a *special* love for Mom.

Okay… to go back to my conditions; Mom showed many symptoms of them. She was paranoid about cleanliness. She would wash meat before putting it in the pan. She would wash the walls of the house periodically. She even brushed my teeth after *I* brushed them until I was six. She obsessed about her children. No one and nothing was ever (almost ever) good enough for us. She was decidedly overprotective.

In fact, when she found out a 5th grader threatened to beat me up, she waited outside the school the next day at dismissal. When Jimmy (the kid) came out, she grabbed him by the collar, pulled him an inch from her face, and said "if you *ever* go near my son Charlie, I will find you!" Jimmy turned sheet white and never bothered me again. Whenever he walked past my mom, he would politely say, "Hello Mrs. St. Cross." You could do that sort of thing back in the mid 1970's and not be arrested.

She was everything to us; loving mother, caregiver, nurse, friend, chef, and protector. She was the whole reason we were a "whole" family in the first place. Dad was a drinker. And when he came home too many nights inebriated, Mom walked up to him with a coffee pot and swung it upside his head. That was her message that his behavior was not acceptable for a family man. He stopped drinking; virtually altogether. It takes a courageous woman to do that to a 6' tall, big, powerful, drunken ex-Marine. She was a strong woman, especially when it came to the benefit of her kids.

While my Dad was intellectually limited, my mother was brilliant. In the late 1940's she simply had no academic opportunity in an old fashioned Italian family. Knowing exactly where she was directing her family was all that mattered to her. She cared nothing for herself. We went on no vacations, as she saved for our college. I mean no vacations ever, not one. We knew no different, so it didn't faze my sister, brother, or I. She made all the decisions and made sure we wanted for nothing. She wore old shabby dresses and a coat with a hole in it. She spent hours cutting endless coupons. She *cut her own hair* to save money. And eventually she sent two boys to college on my father's top salary of $27,000 a year…with NO loans. Hard to believe I know. She was incredible. And yes, don't forget that she did this while suffering from both OCD and Depression. Extraordinarily incredible. Again, THE Greatest Generation.

If it is true that OCD and Depression is passed on through the old double helix, then my kooky older sister and I got it from my parents. (My brother is normal. Can you believe our disappointment?) But, that was only one negative thing amongst hundreds of wonderful things they gave us. All I can say is that when I die, if my kids miss me half as much as I miss my parents, I'll consider my life a success. I still pray to them. If it's possible, I know they are listening. I still ask for their help. If it's possible, I know they give it. I wish every day to see them again. If it's possible, I know someday we'll be together again. God bless them.

Patient: "Doctor, help me. I think I'm a dog."

Psychologist: "I'll see what I can do for you. Relax. Lie down on the couch."

Patient: "I can't. I'm not allowed on the furniture."

Chapter 12b (not 13)

**You're Normal If You Do These Things; I Do Them and I'm......
You Know What I Mean**

People with OCD tend to exhibit certain behaviors. (14) I sat down this afternoon and really concentrated in an effort to think of all the odd things I do that can be attributed to my condition. A few I possibly do just because I'm peculiar, but who's to say? I…….

1) Keep things that are of little or no value just because of sentiment. I do this because I associate them with a happy experience. This may be because I have a limited amount of happy experiences. I am depressed you know. Some may say…. oh, that's called hoarding. It's not hoarding. I don't go for volume, but rather quality regardless of how trivial the item.

2) I crave order (I just misspelled that and typed, "I crave odor." That would be really be creepy. I'm glad I don't have *that*

condition.) But to best describe "order", I mean I like things in line or symmetrical. Shoes on the floor should be on the proper side and evenly placed. Forks in the drawer should all be "tine up" and facing the same way. Pill bottles in the medicine cabinet should all be label out going from large to small, left to right respectively.

3) Numbers are important, and counting is a big deal for me. Do you remember The Holy Grail when they say "The magic number is three. Thou shall not count to one, nor two, unless proceeding to three. Four is out!" I like to do things three times. Example; I press the soap dispenser three times when I wash my hands (see the next habit). Why? Because of the importance of my wife, older son, and younger son. In turn, we go through an exorbitant amount of soap. When I get a glass of water for my son I have to fill and empty the glass three times before I present it to him. This way I know there is no dust in the glass.

4) O.K. that brings me to a biggy; the washing of the hands. I wash my hands A LOT. This is one habit that most people recognize as a symptom of OCD. Well, they're right. I wash my hands around, and this is an estimate 15-20 times a day. Sanitizer does not do it for me. The majority of those times are not because they're dirty. Most of them

are because I've touched an object that has a negative association for me. So, to exonerate that, I wash it away in the sink. You could say that most of the time I'm washing away a negative thought and not germs. On the extremely elusive "bright side", I don't get sick much. Hah! Glass half full. Or you could say I'm *sick* all the time. Glass half empty.

5) Routines are popular with OCD patients. Sometimes I need to follow a routine, like the order in which I make an omelet for my son for breakfast. But this isn't very prominent for me. I hear it's quite a deal for some other OCD sufferers.

I'm not nearly done talking about my(our) problems. I just was tired of writing about them. I figured that, if I was tired of writing about them, then you must be tired of reading about them. The last thing I want is for this book to be boring. So, if we have to cover some boring things the least I can do is split it up into two chapters. That way you can feel a sense of accomplishment by finishing Chapter 12b (not 13), go to bed, and continue reading the next day. I'm all about my readers. Stick with me. We're nearly through all my "exotic" habits. I prefer exotic over strange. Don't you?

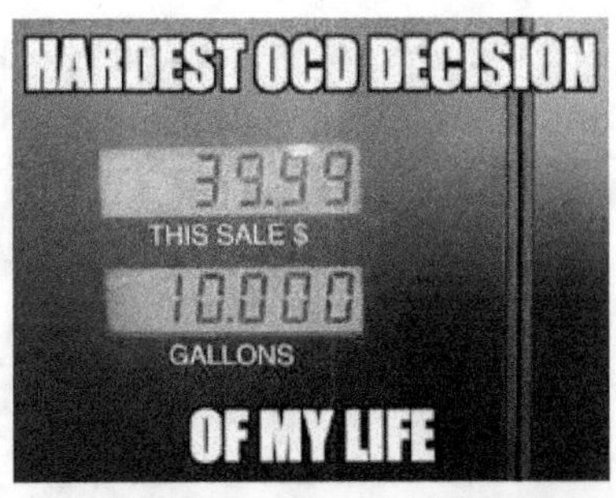

Chapter 14 (not 13b)
I Hope You Enjoyed the Intermission,
But There's Enough Material Here for a
Symposium

6) Okay, here's a combo eccentricity. I, when leaving the house, need to check that appliances are off. I have to check the toaster, the coffee maker, the dishwasher, the dryer, the washer, the microwave, etc. And the twist is that I have to look at them *three times*. See how I can double up on my idiosyncrasies? Checking AND counting simultaneously. It's like I'm a skater performing a double axel followed directly by a triple salchow. That takes talent. I just watched the winter Olympics. ;-) I'm definitely not sure of what damage an unsupervised, rogue microwave can do. But, we're not gonna find out while I'm on duty.

7) Next…a twist to checking….I know we've already touched on this so I'll be

brief…..doors have to be checked to make sure they are closed and locked. The number of times they must be checked is usually three. But it can sometimes depend directly upon whether there are people home. The fear is about the chance that someone can enter and hurt someone, not about whether they will steal the TV or stereo. For me, three of course is the minimum, much more if someone's home.

8) Fear of harm is a distinct OCD symptom for me. I don't like walking across the room with knives from the dishwasher to the table if family is in the room. I create unrealistic scenarios where I trip over something and the knives go flying. I'm super careful when I'm forced to handle sharp objects and people are around, to an extreme degree. Some OCD'ers have worries about hurting themselves. I don't. I don't even wear my seatbelt. I'm bound to get a ticket sooner or later. Arthur Jr., my brother, is a police officer in my town, so he could bail me out right? I bet we'll soon see.

9) One habit I've graduated from is "touching" objects in a certain way. When I was younger, if I dragged my hand against a door knob, I'd get the feeling that I "left a piece of me there". *Now* you really are starting to grasp the degree of insanity I possess, aren't you? Jealous??? I'd have to

go back and re-touch the door knob to "retrieve what I had left there." If I didn't I'd feel anxiety and depression. (12) Yeah, this one is over the top. But some people with OCD exhibit this habit. Remember, I don't anymore. I really don't. Never ever. I swear. Promise. (maybe sometimes) I am just generically insane and no longer one of those people who think they've "left a piece of themselves" on a door knob. No, I'm not one of them, they scare me. LOL

10) A habit I think all people demonstrate to some degree is avoidance. A common, notice I didn't say normal, person may avoid the basement because that's where the washing machine is next to a pile of dirty clothes. Going down there would lead to the feeling of obligation to do the laundry. A person with OCD might avoid being the last to leave the house, so they could logically reason that they should not have to be the one to do the required checking. Get it? But avoidance is universal. OCD just puts a psychological spin on it.

11) A good deal of people with OCD have a constant need for reassurance. That's going to be a chapter. That's a good idea, right? I mean, don't you think so too? Do you agree? LOL Don't you like this "Coming Attractions" format? So exciting!

12) People who are OCDers sometimes have an excessive religious focus. I'm going to let this one slide until later because I want to devote another chapter to it. God deserves at least a chapter, yes?

13) Contamination is usually a stout fear for OCDers. Yet another one I want to expend a chapter on.

14) I'm putting down another one for two reasons. I have OCD….. you don't end with the number 13. Secondly, it's very true. People with OCD lose their confidence. Some, or in my case, nearly all of it. I have three college degrees but am afraid I'll screw up writing a check. It is sad and disabling. The simplest decisions overwhelm me. I'm not the man I used to be. I was so much more. Impressive even. I someday hope to return to be the *late great me*. (4)

While reading the newspaper, a man came across an article about a beautiful actress and model who married a boxer who was not noted for his IQ.

"I'll never understand," he said to his wife, "why the dumbest jerks get the most attractive wives."

His wife replied: "Thank you, dear!"

Chapter 15
Have Gun, Will Travel

What is a trigger? A trigger is usually a word and sometimes action that sets your OCD into motion and slides you into an irrational thought connection mode. (1) Let me clarify by giving you an example. A haircutter was cutting my hair and he had an accent. Making conversation I said, "I noticed your accent, where are you from originally?" He said, "Colombia". Well, as strange as it may seem, that was a trigger for me.

You see I once knew a man who visited Colombia. That same man lost his house and had to move into a smaller, shabby one. I remembered this and thought, "how terrible." And as strange and bizarre as it sounds, I thought. "what if I wish that for my family?" *It's crazy, it's ludicrous, it's absurd, it's ridiculous!* I don't wish for that! But what if I *do*? That is my doubting mechanism kicking in. Maybe by just thinking of it indicates that that's what I truly want. I *don't* wish we lose our house. But, what if I *do*? It's illogical and preposterous, but it lingers there in the center of my mind. Again, this is called a doubting mechanism and it can be a bastard. I know 2+3 doesn't equal 4. *But what if I'm wrong and it does???* So nuts, so real for us.

Back to the Colombian thought. I think, "How awful I am. What a horrible person I am." The fact that that thought entered my mind makes me feel incredibly guilty. (15) I shouldn't live. I don't deserve to. This is a prime example of a "trigger." The word Colombia led me to want to die. Connections. How many connections did I have to make to get from that trigger to wishing just to die?

And once again, a trigger can be anything. It could be a word, a song, a place, an action. But the longer you live with OCD the more triggers you collect. You get to the point where just getting out of bed is accepting the challenge of getting through the day without encountering any of scores of triggers you have developed. After 49 years of OCD, triggers are everywhere for me, and in upcoming chapters I'll be advising you as to how to deal with them.

Triggers cause OCD patients to want to *stay* in bed. If you don't interact with people they can't say something that will "pull" (I coined that term 😊) a trigger. Having no life experiences, eliminates the possibility that an action will "pull" a trigger. Not reading anything, ensures you won't "pull" a trigger. There are many times I won't start a conversation with someone for this very reason. I might not go to the dry cleaners for this very reason.

I might not listen to the radio for this very reason. But the connections you make in the process of experiencing the spiraling downward that a trigger causes are indicative of the overactivity of the brain an OCD patient exhibits. See the scan of the brain scan on the back cover of the book. (22)

People with OCD are, as I've said, generally very sharp people. (8) Finding small ways to vaguely connect diverse thoughts and experiences takes smarts. It's the kind of smart you don't want to have, but it's there nonetheless. Be proud of that. Colombia sucks anyway. It's all about drugs, crime, coffee, and the Miss Universe Pageant. But it's also a trigger for me. BANG!

A psychiatrist was conducting a group therapy session with four young mothers and their small children. "You all have obsessions," he observed.

To the first mother he said, "You are obsessed with eating. You even named your daughter Candy."

He turned to the second mom. "Your obsession is money. Again, it manifests itself in your child's name, Penny."

He turned to the third mom. "Your obsession is alcohol and your child's name is Brandy."

At this point, the fourth mother got up, took her little boy by the hand and whispered, "Come on, Dick, let's go home."

Chapter 16
Pull the Trigger

As we've thoroughly discussed, often there are triggers that cause your mind to direct itself toward one of your obsessions. It can be best understood metaphorically. Your brain is like an expansive filing cabinet. Inside it are countless extended memories, single life moments, and thoughts. I define extended memories as remembering that, *Dad always used the take me to baseball games.* Single life moments are more like, *I remember when Derek Jeter hit that homerun.* Thoughts are just *seeing yourself swinging a baseball bat.* But as you can see on the comparative scans of the brain on the back cover of this book (22), a person with OCD does not have the mind of a common person.

A common person has extended memories, single life moments, and isolated thoughts as well. But an OCD sufferer connects them in an irrational, frenetic, and often disturbing way. He or she even connects them when there is no "sane" connection. (15) For instance, maybe being dragged off to baseball games was a bad experience. I never said that the memories, moments, and thoughts had to be positive. Perhaps their dad drank heavily at these games and turned what would have been a good experience into a bad one. Within that memory of baseball games is eating hot dogs as so often baseball game attendees do.

Now an OCD person years later may connect hotdogs to baseball, baseball to their father, and their father to drunkenness. Due to this distorted connection of memories and thoughts, an OCD person will at all cost avoid aisle 2 at the supermarket. Why? Because that's where the hot dogs are. They know that hotdogs are a trigger for them; a trigger to something hurtful or painful. To them hotdogs are a direct connection to their father's drunkenness. Crazy, I know, but very real to that person.

Why does this happen? I refer back to the scan of an OCD person's hyperactive brain activity. Their brain never stops seeking out connections, no matter how contorted. There is an imbalance in the brain chemicals serotonin and glutamate and an overactivity of neuro-transmitters. (22) These play a huge part in OCD. In fact, when I first started on OCD medications, I slept throughout the day and night for almost a week. My mind, for the very first time in my life was at relative rest.

The best thing to do to reduce the number of triggers you have, according to the psychiatric community, is immersion. In other words, expose yourself to these triggers until they fail to cause you anxiety. (17) But the key is to do it on your own terms. Set small goals for yourself. If the beach for instance is a trigger, start by driving to the beach. Just sit in the parking lot and read a book. Accept the uncomfortableness you feel knowing that you are working toward progress. After a few times of this, bring a chair and sit on the sand. You will feel tremendous anxiety the first time but it will dissipate the more you do it. Soon you'll be in the water and slowly easing away from the beach being a trigger. In psychiatric terms this is called CBT or cognitive behavioral therapy. I call it immersion therapy because it is a more accurate description. But, again, it is much more effective and less painful to do it on your own and on your own terms, i.e. when you think you can handle it without crumbling.

The fewer triggers you have, the less obsessive thoughts you will have, and therefore less anxiety and the dire need to give in to your compulsions. This is a strategy that you can do at your own pace and not on the days you know will be especially challenging for you. It puts you in control and gives you a sense of empowerment that you can direct your own healing.

A husband and wife have four sons. The oldest three are tall with red hair and light skin while the youngest son is short with black hair and dark eyes.

The father was on his deathbed when he turned to his wife and said, "Honey, before I die, be totally honest with me: Is our youngest son my child?"

The wife replied, "I swear on everything that's holy that he is your son."

With that, the husband passed away. The wife muttered, "Thank God he didn't ask about the other three."

Chapter 17
My Bad

Isn't that becoming more and more commonly heard when someone makes a mistake? "My bad.", is exclaimed by the person at fault and they are absolved from any repercussions, penalties, or guilt. "My bad.", and the situation is over, done, fini (that's French, are you impressed?), history. It simply doesn't work that way for me or for many OCD sufferers. Our court of personal law goes much deeper and is significantly less forgiving than the judge and jury that acquits a person who offers a flippant "My bad."

I can't speak for every OCD sufferer, but I know I'm speaking for a decent number. You see, when I make a mistake, I need to know why. Why?

Because OCD sufferers live with racing, unwanted, distracting thoughts. Mistakes are frequently made because the person in question is mentally distracted in some way. (3)

We've all almost gone through a stop sign because our minds were on something other than safe driving. Now, if I were to almost go through a stop sign, a mental investigation would ensue. If I could clearly remember that my mind was on the groceries I had to pick up for dinner, I would be acquitted. That's a normal thought that unfortunately and temporarily drew my attention away from the road. In other words, I would be okay with that.

However, if what drew my attention away from driving was a stray, unwanted thought that I could in any way relate to my obsession or obsessions, I would fall into a panic. I would desperately feel the immediate need to do the compulsion that would make me feel better. I guarantee you the ritual would not be as simple as a "My bad." The ritual could manifest itself in countless ways. Let me give you a single example, but one of the exact nature of missing a stop sign.

In a session I attended, there was a gentleman who shared that he did that very thing (rolled through a stop sign) when his thoughts raced and his obsessions distracted him. He imparted that his method of absolution, his compulsion, was the following. He had to, for the rest of the day, count to ten when he stopped at a stop sign.

The ritual could have been anything, but this was his. No matter if he was all alone at an intersection or there were six people honking behind him. (Relevant tangent here: I originally wrote "five people behind him. ", but had to change it. My mother died on the 15th of October and whenever at all possible I avoid fives; just one of my obsessions, sorry) Anyway, this man actually counted ten Mississippi at every ensuing stop sign he encountered. To hell with the people behind him.

On the surface, and to someone who doesn't have the condition, it may seem a humorous circumstance; a timid soul counting carefully, cowering behind the wheel as people behind him shouted, swore, and honked. But try, just try to put yourself in his shoes for a moment. Imagine the panic, fear, and shame he felt. It must have been humiliating. Try not to laugh. Pity him.

If I were having a day when I couldn't completely suppress or even postpone my ritual, I would get in contact with my wife as soon as possible, reiterate the event and mistake to her. Then I'd explain to her what was going through my mind, no matter how awkward or embarrassing. And then await her response. In a case as presented above. She would say, "You thought what you did because you have a psychological condition that distorts your thoughts. Don't look for meaning, there is none. No one was hurt. You need to let it go." I know this because she's had over 25 years' experience helping me manage my condition. That's why she's my special person. I could hear her voice, "Let it go." She coined that phrase long before Elsa from Frozen ever did. Princess Sofia…has a nice ring to it. But that would make me Prince Charles and that title is taken. Damn! I'm so much better looking than him, yet he gets to be the prince. Life is not Disney.

Chapter 18
Are You Sure I'm Sure?

Reassurance. Often, An OCD person craves reassurance. It could be reassurance about any number of things. It often is reassurance about a decision, no matter how small. (4) That's why, as I've mentioned before, it is very hard for me to go shopping alone. I have to make decisions and choices that are very hard for me to do independently. When I'm with my wife I'll ask for reassurance about something as simple as if the can of pineapple I chose was okay.

Reassurance can also come in the form of looking for "comforting" after doing a certain action. Me: "I sent the check to the oil company that you left on the desk. Is that alright?" Sofia: "Of course." I'm sure she'd like to follow that with, "you half-wit!" But she loves me far too much for that. And she understands my needs.

Reassurance can also be required by an OCD person for something intangible; like a feeling. Say Sofia's sister does something that really ticks me off. I am temporarily pissed at her. But I know she is a good person. Me: "I don't hate your sister, do I?" Sofia: "No, of course you don't. You're just angry right now. And your condition is not allowing you to have perspective." That special person, if schooled correctly in the machinations of the mind of someone with OCD, can diffuse a meltdown using the right words.

In the car, on our way off somewhere, I may ask Sofia if I shut the stove. Now believe me, I know I shut the stove because I checked it three times. But on some days, for whatever reason, my doubting mechanism (as mentioned previously) asserts itself and I think, "But what if I didn't shut the stove? The house would burn down. I could never forgive myself. My God, I better confirm that I shut the stove with Sofia. I know I shut it, and I know I checked it, but there is too much to lose, yup, I'll ask Sofia." Reassurance.

Directions:

1) Open cap. Sanitize. Close cap.
2) Open cap. Sanitize. Close cap.
3) Make sure cap is firmly closed.
4) Recheck cap.
5) Ask yourself if you think it's really closed.
*6) Ask someone else if <u>they</u> think the cap is really
   closed.*

Chapter 19
Contamination:
MC Hammer Was So Right!
(clue: His most famous song)

Okay, glad you got it. First of all, you may consider
something "contaminated" just because you
associate it with something negative. In school I
hated Spanish and wouldn't bring my Spanish book
in my room at home, because I considered it
contaminated. But most thoughts of contamination
are physical. You could say I should have handled
this with the washing of the hands habit. But it is
ever so slightly different. You may only see the
difference if you're OCD yourself. You might
claim I should have put this with the avoidance
conversation. But, this is more than that.
Contamination *could* be as simple as not wanting to
brush along a car in a parking lot. But it can develop
and evolve into something so much more complex.

If you're *good* at it, (and I am, thank you) it's all about connections. (4) Follow me here. I'm at the doughnut and coffee session after church (no this is not the religion chapter). The man behind the "doughnut line" table throws something away in the trash bin. But then he turns around and hands me a napkin for my doughnut! Well the napkin is contaminated because he handled it after touching the trash bin. Not knowing what to do I pick up a doughnut with it. (what else can you do when you're in a damned doughnut line!) Well, now clearly the doughnut is contaminated.

As an aside, I see someone I know and they start up a conversation. They are talking, I am talking, they are laughing, I am laughing, they are drinking their coffee, I am drinking my coffee, they are eating a doughnut, and I am standing there not eating my undeniably contaminated doughnut thank you. Clearly, he must be wondering (and I'm just making an educated guess), "what the hell does he plan to do with that doughnut? He's holding it between his thumb and forefinger like a piece of freakin' china. Why does one get a doughnut if he doesn't want to *eat* a doughnut?" Well, after the "Give my best to the wife and kids.", I get away and can ditch this tainted ring of dough and accompanying napkin. I successfully do that without even touching the little flip door of the trash receptacle. I have valuable experience in matters such as these. ☺

Wait, now I've got to wash my hands, which is a whole other challenge since I'll need to use a paper towel to shut the faucets and open the door when I leave the restroom. I already know it's dicey that I'll make it through that unscathed. So, I turn around and my son suddenly hands me his religious education book. Well…guess…what. Now the damn *book* (or should I say darn, we're doing a church story here.) is contaminated.

Fine, the whole morning is shot to H-E-double hockey sticks. (think about it…and…you got it!) My son will come back at some point for his book, which will contaminate him. I'm stuck! I won't impose my psychological dysfunctions on my kids. Anyway, *you* try and get a 9-year-old to carefully shut faucets with paper towels. Not gonna happen. This is just going to be one where I have to internalize the worry. It'll bother me until something bigger comes around. I could have gotten my own gosh darn napkin!

In a psychiatrist's waiting room two patients are having a conversation.

One patient says to the second patient, "Why are you here?"

The second patient answers, "I'm Napoleon, so the doctor told me to come here."

The first patient is curious and asks, "How do you know that you're Napoleon?"

The second patient responds, "God told me I was."

At this point, the first patient stands up and shouts, "NO I DIDN'T!"

Chapter 20
Hello God…Charles…Charles St. Cross… Yes, I'll Hold… I'm *What* Number in the Queue?

Don't you wonder what it would be like if God wasn't OMNIPRESENT and he had to take prayers one by one. It would be almost as bad as the DMV on a Saturday morning. I'm sure Jesus would be on a line helping. Maybe the saints would be on staff. But if you really had to talk to the big guy you'd be on the queue forever. You may not live long enough to get to speak to God at all. At least then if you died you could go up to heaven and seek out customer service; maybe file a complaint. Is that sacrilege, filing a complaint against God? Hard questions I know. These are things you'd like to ask

God about, but whose gonna wait on the phone for that long?

I go to church pretty much every week with my family. I pray to God. I pray to my parents. I pray every night. I worry I'll mess up the prayer because of the distraction of a stray unwanted thought, of course, but I do it nonetheless. If you've read my previous book you know that I've done everything that could fall under the religious umbrella to try and transcendentally cure myself.

Since this is covered in my first book I'll be very concise. I've gone to faith healers. I've gone to exorcists. I've gone to Portugal to see a priest who had a "special" connection with God. I've seen religious "experts" who had me bathe in special bath crystals, bleach, suspicious liquids; all to chase the bad spirits from my body. One wanted me to buy a $14,000 "vessel", a *tabernacle*, (really just an ornate vase with a door, without even a lock, like an evil spirit couldn't escape a vase, my cat can get out of his carry case and he doesn't even have opposable thumbs, he's not even an evil cat, mean spirited sometimes but…. sorry) or a vase in which to place the evil spirit she said occupied me. By the way, she wanted a bankers check. Right there is a red flag that she was no instrument of the Lord. I know the Lord accepts personal checks. I put one in the basket every Sunday. He never sends them back.

Nothing that I've done has had any effect on my mental health. Do I blame God for what I endure?

No. I more blame myself for the sins I've committed over my almost 49 years, and the possibility that God is punishing me in some way for my behavior. Have I sinned any more than the next guy? I don't know. I guess it depends on the next guy. Jimmy Carter once said that if they put people in jail for their thoughts, we'd all be in jail. The Clinton's have tested this theory to the extreme and they've never experienced any repercussions for what they've done.

We've all sinned. All I know is that I do believe in an afterlife and a God. And God says the more we suffer here on earth the more glorious our afterlife will be. If this is true, I'm definitely going to have a big screen television with surround sound up there. I'm just hoping it will be "up there" and not in the opposite direction.

There's got to be a heaven, because I just have to see my mother and father again. I won't let myself think any differently. I also am sure they can't help me, because neither my mother nor father would ever allow me to suffer the way I do each day if they could help it at all. I'll continue to pray. Whether it will ever do any good, who's to say. I have a current deal with God that he can have me suffer as much as need be as long as he protects and blesses my wife and boys. They're all that matters. They're everything. For now, however, the title of the chapter in my previous book still stands. *I Talked to God and God Said…Nothing Special.*

Patient: "Doctor, I'm having memory problems. I can't remember what I had for breakfast this morning, what I wore yesterday, the names of my grandkids, or even the where I put my keys."

Doctor: "Is there anything in particular that you can remember?"

Patient: "My password to my computer."

Doctor: "Why do you think that is?"

Patient: "I've made my password "incorrect", so every time I type something, the computer says "incorrect" and I remember!"

Chapter 21
Depression? I Prefer Despair.
TomAto...Tomahto

Depression can stand alone as a debilitating psychological condition. However, it is very often found partnered with other conditions, OCD being a prominent one. Depression is often called a black hole. This analogy is accurate in several ways. When you are in deep Depression you do literally feel as though life is just darkness, lacking any light at the end of the tunnel. A person who has acute Depression is hard to reach. You would be hard pressed to find any life blessing that the depressed person cannot obscure with dark thought, no matter how remote or irrational. (18)

I honestly feel my Depression is the devious sidekick of my OCD. As I've said, I believe my OCD is the chicken to Depression's egg. Some doctors I've had have tried to treat them separately. I personally don't think that's realistic. One Ivy League institute affiliated doctor thought he could tackle them separately and decided to focus on my Depression first. He was of the belief that ECT or Electro Convulsive Therapy would greatly improve my feelings of Depression. This therapy is commonly known as Electric Shock Treatment. This is a story I shared partially in my last book. But I think it bears review as the ramifications of the outcome still haunt me today.

When he told me his plan I was surprised because I thought this treatment was something of the past that had long since been disproven as a legitimate type of treatment. I mean, it is essentially putting nodes on the forehead of the patient and sending electricity through their brain, thus causing a brief seizure. After undergoing a number of treatments, I felt no different. Their response was to add another node to the other side of my head. If one doesn't do the trick, try two right? Simple math that any Ivy League affiliated doctor can deduce. Well there still was no change. I began reading about the procedure and "they" say (they in this case was the medical community I suppose, because I couldn't find a specific study to site) that most people feel positive effects after only 6 to 12 treatments. I was about to go to my **29th**!

At that point I began to think for myself. (what a novel concept) Why trust an esteemed Ivy League doctor who is pointlessly electrocuting you three times a week, robbing you of your short-term memory when you can decide your own treatment? I have three university degrees, none of them medical, but that's only one less than him! I concluded that this path was something less than "effective" for me. I never went to that 29th treatment. I told them they could offer my slot to some other poor soul and that I'd be looking for another physician, one whose frontline of defense against Depression wasn't inducing electrically based seizures in their patient's brains.

What do I have to show for my faith in the Ivy League affiliated hospital I placed my faith in? Well, my short-term memory never returned to its "pre-treatment" state. To this day I have trouble remembering things that happened up to a few weeks ago. I can't retain information from the morning to the evening. I'm not the same, and not for the better. I won't disclose which hospital let this electric shock treatment go on for almost three to five times longer than it should have. Did I yet mention that I live near New Haven, CT? No? Well, I guess I *forgot*.

Doctor to Patient: "Remember, saying the same thing over and over again and expecting different results is the definition of insanity."

Patient: "It's also called parenting."

Chapter 22
Pardon Me While I Think the Worst

Depression for me can best be exemplified by my feelings during "happy times". My family is my grand savior. When I feel good, there's a 100% chance it's because I'm doing something with them. Wait…is 100% a chance? It's really a surety, right? 99.99999 percent is still a chance. But 100% is a guarantee. I like math; philosophy too. Do I get extra points for combining them? Boredom points you say??? Oh, I see. I'll keep moving then.

Say I'm in the pool with my son and we're playing ball. He's having a great time and I should be too. Being a depressive person I'm not in the moment enjoying my son and the activity in which we're involved. I'm thinking this:

"My God I love my son. And I love playing with him. But this activity can't last forever. Our time to play together isn't endless. Eventually we'll be called inside to shower and go to bed. The day will be over. The fun we had will have passed. Those same exact moments can never happen again. My son is growing up and this is now just one less time I'll get to play with him. One less time, as a child,

he'll want to play with me. My God before I blink he'll be looking for colleges. What if he wants to live away for college. God forbid. I can't go on for weeks or even days without seeing him. But there is nothing I could do to prevent time from passing. It is an endless ever flowing river. As Sting says in his song <u>All This Time</u> , "the river flows, endlessly, to sea". I am so sad."

You see, depression is like an evil fluid. (Can fluids be inherently evil? I once had a shot of Portuguese "moonshine" call aguardente ("intense water", literally made out of the vines and skins of grapes and not the flesh of the grapes themselves). I was never sicker. I would classify that libation as distinctly "evil". I'm such a lightweight. Following the analogy of Depression as a fluid, if poured on something it will seep into any crack or crevice possible. Bad thoughts lead to more bad thoughts, exponentially. It will leave virtually no area untouched, unaffected. That is why a black hole is such an appropriate parallel. Depression pulls you in as does a black hole. The more you think as a depressive the more it will lead to depressing thoughts. They multiply. (16) The closer you get to a black hole the greater the gravitational pull it has on you. In both cases, there seems to be no escape. Eventually you conclude the quest for happiness is futile.

The head psychiatrist decides it's time to see whether some patients are ready to leave the "hospital" so he takes one to a room where there is a large, <u>empty</u> swimming pool, and a diving board overhanging it.

He takes the patient to the edge of the board and says: "Jump!" The patient jumps and breaks both his legs and is carried away.

The next patient is taken up and after the same injunction, jumps and breaks both her arms and is carried away.

The last patient is taken up and told to jump and he refuses.

The head psychiatrist says, "Congratulations! You have passed the sanity test and are free to leave. But tell me, asks the doctor out of curiosity, why did you refused to jump."

The patient replies, "I can't swim."

Chapter 23
How Smart I Am

Truth be told, I'm not any smarter than anyone else with this condition. Although, there has been some correlation between high intellect and having OCD. As a shot to my ego, results from this research have varied. Me…. I just have decades of experience with the condition and the treatments that go along with them. We have covered lots of OCD symptoms and related topics over the last 17 chapters. Alphabetically (is there any other proper way) we've discussed avoidance, checking, confidence, contamination, counting, DNA, doctors, fears, keeping things, medications, numbers, order, reassurance, religion, routines, shopping, touching, and washing. I have been to endless therapists through my doctors, partial-hospitalization, and full hospitalization.

I feel the need here to differentiate between the latter two. With full hospitalization, you actually live in the psychiatric unit. The rooms on one side are for the women and the rooms on the other side are for the men. Like camp, right??? No. Not *at all* like camp! "Camp Insanity" maybe! Scary men. Scarier women. I did not belong there and my doctor at the time should have known. I admitted myself, desperate for any help. Instead of cluing me in on what to expect, he actually left for vacation the following day. How could I go wrong with such dedicated and invested medical support? What an incompetent clown.

I was an average person who had the misfortune of having two conditions that were affecting his life to the point of ruining it. I was acutely depressed, and full of anxiety with OCD. Outwardly, I was just an introverted very sad man. Conversely, my co-patients at this hospital included heavy drug addicts who were violent criminals, people with disassociative identity disorder whose personality would turn from docile to vicious frequently, people who talked to themselves at full volume as they walked in circles, and one man who tried to commit suicide but failed. Instead he pummeled both his parents near death with a baseball bat.

I did not belong there. I was absolutely terrified every minute as orderlies physically wrestled other patients to the ground as they tried to escape the ward. I woke one morning with another patient standing directly over my bed just staring at me. It was, without hesitation, the ten most terrifying days of my life. I never returned to the psychiatrist who allowed me to go through that. My only hope is that he finds himself inside that ward one day. Not enough bad things can happen to this alleged "doctor". I never said I was forgiving.

Teens had their own unit. Your day was scheduled so you could attend therapy workshops throughout the great majority of the day. You had meals, and if you weren't an "escape attempt" risk, you were allowed in the courtyard for dinner. Not that you could escape from the courtyard anyway. It was fenced in. I'm talkin' about a fence that would make President Trump proud; like 20 feet high. No one was leaving the Mexican Psychiatric Ward.

In contrast, partial-hospitalization was just that. You're in the hospital for only part of the day (large part), in at 9:00 a.m. and out at 4:00 p.m. Again, your day was packed with a great diversity of therapies. You only took an hour off at midday for lunch. Oddly enough, no one cared who might be planning an escape. During one really tedious therapy session it crossed my mind. But it wouldn't have been an honest challenge. No fences. LOL Anyway, the bottom line of this story is that everyone there was sane; just troubled. It was relatively productive, I must say.

Seriously, I could literally open my own therapy center given the amount, width, and breadth of the therapies I've been taught. That's actually not a bad idea. I'm going to consider it.

A man was walking in the street one day when he was brutally beaten and robbed.

As he lay bleeding, a psychologist, who happened to be passing by, tackles the offender and subdues him.

The psychiatrist takes out his phone to make a call.

The injured man says, "Are you calling 911?"

The psychiatrist say's, "No, I'm calling my office, this man needs help!"

Chapter 24
Hey, He Said He'd Get to That!...
or Loose Ends

There are some loose ends in this book that I'd like to handle now; issues of Obsessive Compulsive Disorder and Depression that were mentioned previously that I promised I'd address. Well here I go. These are my own personal recommendations as someone with nearly a half century of experience with Obsessive Compulsive Disorder and Depression. I promised I'd address them, and will to the best of my ability given my life experience. The keyword for the chapter: LIMITS.

Let's start with the symptom of excessive order. When you see shoes on the floor that are askew, or cans on the kitchen shelf that are in disarray. You need to be all about baby steps and working toward where you want to be. Set small goals. For instance, if those cans are really bothering you, fix them, but only fix one shelf. There are generally three shelves in a kitchen cabinet. Pick the one you want and rearrange it with the internal contract that you won't touch the other two shelves. To hell with them. Maybe fix a second shelf tomorrow, but for today you are setting parameters for yourself. You are setting and following a limitation. Your compulsion has taken a hit. You are not totally giving in. That deserves points. Do it.

Checking is the next compulsion. You may take several minutes to leave the house because you are checking everything is as it should be before you leave. Let's start with what's sane. Check the doors. It's normal. You should know the doors are locked if you are leaving your home. Other forms of checking are different. Has anyone used the stove that day? If the answer is no, then you can't check the knobs to make sure they are on off. If they were left on, the fiery catastrophe would have happened by now. It is not logical to check the stove unless someone has been using it.

Lights. Look around. Do you see any lights on? If yes, then shut them. This is simply to minimize your electricity bill. But do not do a walkthrough of the house to check every light. Don't go to the basement, the downstairs family room, the upstairs bedrooms. It is not healthy to do this, it is obsessive. If something is on, so what. Lights stay on all day sometime and nothing happens. The bulbs will not explode and cause a fire. Nothing will touch the bulb and go aflame. The house will not burn down. Leave it alone.

Groceries are the next topic. Make the decision that you will only check things with a very limited shelf life, i.e. perishables. Check the milk, eggs, sour cream, and bread. But do not check the cookies. Do not check the apple juice. Do not check the vitamins. These things have expiration dates on them because its required by law. But they are expirations that are multiple months ahead. You will have used the product by then. And a box of cornflakes that have an expiration date of 10 months ahead are just as good and taste the same as a box of cornflakes that are 9 months ahead. Only check dates on items when it is sensible to check them.

Finding a good doctor is not an easy question to answer, because a good doctor for one person is not a great choice for another. My advice here is that you should not feel shackled to the doctor you are currently using. If that doctor is not helping you progress with your conditions or is strong-arming you to do things that make you uncomfortable or is making your symptoms worse, try another psychiatrist. Make sure however that you find someone who is skilled with manipulating medications to adjust for the feedback you give him/her. Find a doctor that is current with the latest drugs. But ultimately find a doctor you can look in the eye and say, "This cocktail of medications is not working for me. Can we try something else?" without being timid or feeling intimidated. Your doctor, you, and your special person are a team, not a hierarchy.

The act of holding onto sentimental things is our next topic. This is a relatively easy one. Get yourself a box. A reasonably sized one. I have a box the size of one used for copy paper. Keep whatever you want that fits in that box. When the box is full you need to go through it and discard things that are least important to you. I know you crave to keep everything you connect to a happy memory. But space does not provide for this. Remember, even if the item has to leave the box, the memory will live in your heart and mind. And you will be heathier.

Washing hands is probably the most common and well-known symptom of OCD. I follow the following guidelines when my state of mind is able. If you have something on your hands wash them. If you have ketchup on your palm, wash your hands. If you have touched something that is likely to harbor germs, wash them. If you change the cat litter, you've touched something that may convey germs. Wash your hands. If you come home from a day at work or a day working outside, you've touched many things at times when you haven't had the chance to wash your hands. Plus, a great keeper of germs, the steering wheel in your car. Definitely wash them upon arriving home. These are the only instances that I can think would merit washing your hands. The ultimate message is that you should never wash your hands because you have touched something you associate with a negative thought or obsession. If you do, you are fostering a common unhealthy compulsion.

Be brave; if not for you, then for your wife or husband or children. You may feel completely intimidated by the thought of leaving the house one day. THIS is the day to go out. This is the greatest opportunity to deliver a forceful blow to your condition. If you are at the department store and usually avoid aisle 8 because you know you will see a trigger, make it a point to go down that aisle. Pick up the damned item and laugh to yourself, knowing that your anxiety is real to you, but ludicrous to sane life. Do something important ALONE. Do it because you know it is important, has to be done, and maybe very challenging. And the key here is…. don't ask for any reassurance from anyone. Have confidence you've done it correctly. This is a huge strike to your reassurance tendencies. Be brave! Your wife or husband need you to be healthy. Your kids need you to be healthy. You need to be healthy to have a good life. *Be brave.* I know you can do it!

Chicken on psychiatrist's couch: "I'm starting to think I didn't cross the street just to get to the other side. My God, help me doc. Why do you think I crossed it?"

Chapter 25
After All That You Still Have Questions?
OK, So Ask

Explanation:

After my first book, I'm Not Sick, But I'm Not Well: Finding Happiness Despite OCD and Depression, many readers had questions and contacted me through email. At the end of this book I'll give you my contact information so you can do the same. These questions, I'm sure are representative of the questions that traverse the minds of all my readers. That is why I'm taking the time now to respond to them. A good question deserves a good answer. Again, these are the thoughts and beliefs of someone with extensive experience. Here we go…

How can I stop my racing, unwanted thoughts?

Racing, unwanted thoughts are relatively common for a person with OCD. There are two aspects to them that I'd like to address. First, an OCD mind is like a boat with a gaping hole in it on a lake. If the boat is empty, water (thoughts) is going to race in. Secondly, the thoughts that will race in are of the most unwanted kind. The water that comes through that hole will not be clean, clear and, pristine. The water that rushes in is dark and murky and muddy. The thoughts will be thoughts you would least like having. They could be sad memories, they could be of an object or person you have a negative association with, they could be an aspect of yourself that you are ashamed of. Whatever the metaphorical water is, it will be the most, most distasteful kind.

The easy answer to the question as stated above is that you don't *stop thoughts*. They will come and despite the best medications, there will be days when they come fast and furious. But, I would not leave you high and dry. I have a management technique I want to share that will make the thoughts less influential in your life.

As a manner of review, you have a negative, unwanted, stray thought. That is a form of obsession. You are thinking things you don't want to think and the more you try to stop the harder it is to stop. So…. don't try. Take the thoughts as they come. Tell your demons to bring it on! But, and this is a Kardashian sized *but*, make a covenant with yourself. You know you will need to perform the compulsion (or ritual as I like to call it) to absolve yourself of that or those terrible thoughts. The key is to make the commitment to hold off on the ritual until a later time. Yes, I'm saying to live with the discomfort of your terrible, Godforsaken guilt for a designated time. Just do it. If what I say doesn't work I promise I'll go to hell in your place.

When I began this technique, I would set a goal of one hour before I had to do the compulsion. Then I would do it. It's okay. This is what we call progress. Then I set my goal to three hours. And then I would do the compulsion. Then I set my goal for five hours. And you know what??? Sometimes I would forget to do the compulsion. Then I set my goal to bedtime. And yes, more and more, I would forget to do the compulsion. Again, I vow to be completely transparent with you about what we face each day. Sometimes I would need to immediately do the ritual. But, many times, I beat the obsession. I won! I still do this and I still win more than I lose. Given the power of OCD that you and I face every day, I'll take those odds.

Why do I feel the worst in the mornings and nights?

This one is pretty direct. If you are not yet on medication, mornings would be hard for you and your OCD because the entire day lay ahead of you. If you're anything like me the next 12 to 16 hours are an obstacle course that you are about to navigate. You are about to undertake a task that, in your condition is virtually impossible to pull off. You desperately want to get through the day, without behaving embarrassingly in a public place or making a defeating mistake because of your condition. There is no chance, and in your heart and mind you know it, that it's going to happen. You feel anxious, nervous, shaky, and panicked. You need to find a competent doctor and get the proper medication to help you. You can't go this alone.

Now that you have the necessary meds and a doctor to guide you, there are a few things you can do to help. Firstly, What I do is set my alarm for 7 a.m., take my morning medication and then go back to bed. Then when I get up at 8:00 a.m. I feel relatively calmer, less nervous, and experience reduced panic. I am giving my medication a head start. I am buying time for my medication to take effect. If you take all of your anti-anxiety medication in the morning, consider this. Split it to take a portion of it at midday. That way, at 1:00 p.m. or so when you feel yourself start to "drop", you can take that anti-anxiety booster. I would split it as such; 2/3 in the morning, and 1/3 midday. This strategy seems to work for me, so talk to your doctor about giving it a try.

It's hard for me, when I'm supposed to be having a good time, to calm my mind and just enjoy myself. What can I do?

This was a common problem within a group of people at an institute I once attended. A common person can and tends to lose themselves in the moment when they are having fun. This usually does not happen for an OCD sufferer. When an OCDer begins to have fun, their greatest nemesis, their mind, begins to work against them. They fear they will do something wrong to ruin the experience, or even just already begin to lament that the experience will eventually end along with the positive emotion.

A person with OCD must, and I know it sounds strange, retrain themselves to focus on, well........whatever it is they want to focus on. So, this particular doctor running the session said you have to start small. Really small. He said to begin with something like eating a piece of fruit. Take an apple. Notice the little things; the shape, the color, the stem, the taste (I was like ...what??? It tastes like an apple!). But he was referring to the sweetness versus the tartness and junk. It sounds corny but try it. Pick a small moment, brushing your teeth perhaps, and make every effort to just concentrate on the details related to that moment. Eventually, I said eventually, you will be able to focus a little better on a happy moment in your life.

I'm not going to lie to you. Given time, four to five minutes if you're lucky, your stray unwanted thoughts will break through and taint your happiness. That's what OCD does, steal away happiness. But, if we try to use some management techniques like the one introduced here, we can sneak a few minutes of exuberance once in a while. It is a very small battle won. But, given the fierce opponent you face, rejoice in small victories.

I am always unhappy. I feel depressed all the time. What can I do to break this cycle?

"You know, a lot of people are worse off than you!" God don't you hate when people tell you this in the face of Depression? Don't you want to dare them to live one day of their life with your conditions?

Don't want to just smack them upside the head and tell them they have no idea what psychological pain is? Don't you want them to just step out in front of a speeding bus and……. nevermind.

I know how you feel and you are not alone if you can take any solace in that. The first exercise you should do is to sit down and write all the wonderful things in your life. Then make a list of what you truly have to worry about. And I'm talking about major items. On the plus side you may write down the health of your family. On the minus side you might write down the possibility of ruining dinner. Now, I don't guarantee anything here but I'm willing to wager an honest list is going to be weighted towards the plus side. And, as illustrated above, I'd be willing to bet that the minus side will be largely insignificant and merely overblown in your distorted thoughts. Why? Because of the essence of what Depression is. Depression creates the illusion that minor negatives are major problems when they're simply not.

In a group I attended a woman had a bevy of things on her plus side. I'm talking stuff like healthy family, happy family, son in great college, beautiful house, etc. On the negative side was a dishonest friend, taxing college tuition, unable to remember to take pills. These were the things that were distorted in perspective and created the illusion that her world was crumbling down upon her. They were dwarfed by the valuable items on the plus side of her list, but she couldn't see that. This defines what Depression is. It is a condition that distorts your perspective on what's important in life.

You could not put a price on the plus items on her list, but she was giving the common negative items the same weight or credence. If you have a dishonest friend, you end the friendship and find another comrade. If you are struggling to pay those college loans, join the club. Almost everyone struggles and somehow, they get through it. If you are having trouble remembering to take your pills, set a timer on the stove, microwave, phone, alarm clock, whatever.

The point is that these negative that are smothering this poor woman are either insignificant or manageable. Yet, she is letting them overpower any positive emotions that emanate from all the tremendously good things in her life. Don't allow this to happen to you. Whenever you feel sad and depressed, take out your list and read the left side.

Remind yourself of all the ways life has favored you. And make every effort to view the negatives in your life with solid perspective. You may only have one real negative in your life; the cross you bear called Depression. And if we can find a way to manage that, all that's left is the light. All that's left is the meaningful gifts God has granted you. How can you acknowledge them and stay that sad?

I don't know why God has allowed me to suffer so much.

I ask myself this question every night when I go to bed and say my prayers before going to sleep. When I first got really sick I truly thought that my fate was indeed in His hands and that He was making the decision to allow me to suffer. As you know from my first book, I went to my church's priest, faith healers, exorcists, etc.

Yes, I said exorcists but it was nothing like the movie. I didn't levitate, speak in tongues, spit pea soup or anything interesting. They merely said prayers over me, fogged me up with some incense, and literally pushed me down by my forehead. It was to no avail. I guess my possession is permanent. According to one loon, I had an evil presence inside me that was invisible to the naked eye, but visible to a trained battler of demons such as herself. As I mentioned, she claimed she could remove it and put it in an ornate vessel that would have the proper holy security sentinels to keep it contained. The "vessel" would cost me a fortune and her services from then on would be free! Now that's a bargain!

Another faith healer called herself the Grand Holy Mother of the Church of the Disciples. Amazingly enough, she wanted to put my demon in a vessel too. Her price was even higher, but hey, she was a Grand Holy Mother of the Church of the Disciples. I'd like to finish that title with another word beginning with F. Try to guess what it is. It will be fun!!! My brother, the boring sane sibling I have, called her and asked where her church was. She had no answer. He asked if he could have the number of the Father and Nun she reported to. No answer. He asked what holy schooling and career path she had to go through to become Grand Holy Mother of the Church of the Disciples. She hung up. Apparently, she had another call, someone on the other line, maybe God???

Anyway, now that you have a little background of my experience with the religious, let me answer your question. I believe in God. I am Roman Catholic and we go to church almost every Sunday. My kids go to church school. I help pack and deliver food to shelters each November for Thanksgiving. I buy gifts for our church's giving tree each Christmas. I volunteer at the church fair. In summary, I'm not a Holy roller. But, I think I've built up a little goodwill with God for my small deeds of kindness. That said, I don't think it does me any good. Stop here a second. I'm not looking to "get paid back" by God for the little things I do. I just want Him to see me as a decent person.

Despite the great reverence I have for the Lord, I'm now convinced he can't help me. I've suffered long enough to conclude that, if he was going to intervene and "cure" me, he would have done so by now. I know he has over 6 billion people to manage on the earth. But, the word is that he's omnipresent and can be everywhere at once. So, my conclusion is that I am suffering because my DNA has generated a chemical imbalance in my brain, not because of some Holy retribution. This imbalance has caused me to suffer from Obsessive Compulsive Disorder, which enacts another condition called Depression. In other words, God has nothing to do with my suffering. Nor can He do anything to help it. Despite this, I still feel the necessity to cover myself and ask God every night if he could help me out; and more importantly, if He would just take care of my family. That is all I can request.

So please, don't blame God for your condition. Don't expect God to save you from your condition. Please don't go to despicable people, affiliated with a church or not, who say they can save you from your suffering. They take advantage of people in great pain who are desperate. These are despicable, thieving, evil, lowlifes. The truth is that your doctor can't even independently cure you. In fact, (I know how this sounds, but wait for the next paragraph before you slam your book shut) you're not going to be cured.

But have confidence in this; you will, with your doctor's cocktail of medications and your life management strategies and techniques, get *better*. Better enough to lead a largely happy existence. You *can* have significant quality of life. An alcoholic is always an alcoholic, a recovering one. You will always have a chemical imbalance in your brain, but can get yourself to a good place; a happy place. Take your meds, use your strategies, and occasionally say an Our Father, just in case.

When something presses on my mind. How can I make it go away?

Listen, time flies. There is no stopping it. It will advance for the good or the bad. There is a great song by a band called "OK Go" that is called <u>This Too Shall Pass</u>. The video is even better, but I digress. The point it that whatever is bothering you, won't for too long. Something else, good or bad will take its place. Remember, your mind, as an OCDer, is unfortunately a thought machine. It turns out thoughts much, much faster than an average person. Thus, whatever is on your mind now is, for the good or the bad, is temporary. It is part of the parameters, or "by-laws", of your condition. Like it or not.

If a thought is bothering you, you can do the Good Thing or the Bad Thing. "And you want to be good, don't you Danny?" That is a classic line from <u>Caddy Shack</u> when the late, hilarious Ted Knight as the Judge Smails asks Michael O'Keefe as Noonan whether he want to be true to the establishment of the country club or be a rebel in life. I know I'm speaking Greek to those have you who haven't seen the movie, but if you haven't, you absolutely have to. It WILL make you laugh. If you want to call it up now on Netflix I'll wait. 😊

So, you can do the good thing and force yourself to ignore it while building up your tolerance for unwanted thoughts. In other words, tough it out. Or you can give in to the obsession and do the ritual that will make you feel better right now. This is what they call in medical terms, the "bad thing." Don't worry, it's a Latin term. 😊 Building up your tolerance for the bad thoughts and resisting the ritual is what we're shooting for. But I know how hard that can be and I won't judge you if you give in to the compulsion when you are desperate. I've walked in your shoes.

By the way, I can guarantee you will undeniably, eventually have another different thought that will trump it; something that will bother you a little more, thus pushing your first thought into the abyss. I've been there a thousand times. And since your original thought, as most OCD unwanted thoughts are, is inconsequential, it won't come back. That's the good news. The bad news is clearly that you still are wrestling with an unwanted thought, just a new one. Diversity is the spice of life. Does this answer help you? It is the reality of your condition.

However, the theory is that if you continue to ignore your unwanted, ugly thoughts and endure the pain, eventually you *will* stop having them. That being said, this is where I stand. I have an unwanted thought and ignore it as best I can. During the daily routine I sometimes have another unwanted thought that supplants it. I continue to ignore my thoughts (as I said before, often telling myself I'll save the compulsion until later). Bedtime sometimes comes and, if I have kept busy during the day, I fail to recall what was bothering me.

So, the key is to keep busy. A mind filled with "productive" thoughts has no room for inconsequential, insignificant, unwanted thinking. Especially, during the latter part of the day, stay productive. What do I do? I love sports, so I read articles online about my team. I have an acuity for painting, so I sketch out a landscape that I'll paint the next day. I'm OCD, so I'll organize my kids' books alphabetically. Then when bedtime comes sometimes the thought that was unwanted is also unrememberable. Warning, don't be domestic. No laundry or dishes, or vacuuming. With apologizes to those who are "domestic engineers" as a profession, those activities are largely mindless and are a breeding ground for an OCD sufferer's overactive synapses. Now maybe I've answered your question.

Serious Closing Thoughts

No more jokes. No more sarcastic humor. Just me.
I am now finishing writing my second book on the
subject of Obsessive Compulsive Disorder and
Depression. Having had these conditions for so long
and given their complexities, I think I could write
half a dozen more. All I know is that when I write I
try to be as blatantly honest and transparent as
possible. You, the reader, deserve that.

Just because I write about the conflict, doesn't mean
in any way that I've won the battle. The war goes
on for me. I have many days when my conditions
get more than the best of me. There are numerous
times, especially when I'm left alone, that I
cry…hard.

My wife provides me support that I absolutely need
to get out of bed. *My kids* provide me the sunshine
that I absolutely need to occasionally smile. *My
doctor* provides me the medication that I absolutely
need to stabilize my anxiety. This is why in the
previous chapters that I tell you to find "that special
someone" and seek out a skilled doctor. I don't
know where I'd be without this triumvirate of care.

So, I don't write as a victorious conqueror, but
instead as a tired warrior whose learned a lot about
his enemy and how to fight. I want you to know
now what it took me decades to learn. I want to give
you the foresight I wish I had as a miserable young

man. It would have saved me years of heartache and hurt. I still hurt.

Sometimes I try to fool myself and actually embrace it, telling myself it is part of me, I was born to suffer, and I am just faithfully fulfilling my fate as assigned by God. But I know that's just not true. No, I wear no crown of triumph over these unforgiving conditions. I hope to never sound pompous, as I know more than you only because I've suffered and battled longer.

I also write in a large part to entertain my compatriots. I know that smiles and laughs do not come easy, if at all, for sufferers of these two conditions. You lead a hard life and too often people question why you claim anguish when they can't see anything tangible facing you. Your demons are all too real, put appear only to you. If I can make you smile, I feel like I've struck a blow against your adversaries. If I can make you laugh, all the better. I'm sure some of you wonder if you can remember how.

I'm sorry. I'm sorry I can't do more. What I can do, that most others cannot, is honestly sympathize. Because I've walked in your shoes. All I can say to you youngsters in the crowd (and I consider anyone younger than me a youngster) is to heed my advice. My experience and accompanying advice has come through agony, great pain, and hurt. Don't let me have suffered for nothing.

Thank you for reading. And thank you to those who will listen to my words. It's the listeners on whom I'm betting my money. I'd wish you good luck, but you don't need it. You will secure the elements we've discussed to win the war. Congratulations on your impending victory. I wish you peace. May the north you find be true.

Now…after all the importance I've placed on people with our condition finding a smile or laugh wherever they can, there's no way I can leave you without a joke:

There's a man who decides to rent an office on the 19th floor of a building. He was seriously considering the 20th floor, but that's another story.

Take Care…C.K.S.

Appendix

I have taken the liberty to provide you with broad screening surveys for Obsessive Compulsive Disorder and Depression. The survey is a capsulized compilation of various surveys, and I feel serves our purposes here. Now, remember, Depression and especially OCD manifest themselves in a multitude of way for every person. You may not have some of the symptoms that are on these short general surveys. That does not mean you don't show tendencies for OCD and/or Depression. Just take them with a grain of salt. They may give you the reassurance that you don't need to address the minor symptoms that you have. They may also provide the impetus for you to seek out the urgent and critical advice of a doctor to determine methods to improve your everyday life.

If your answers are mostly affirmative, give serious thought to getting help for your problems from your physician who may administer The Yale–Brown Obsessive–Compulsive Scale (Y-BOCS) and/or the National Institute of Mental Health-Global Obsessive–Compulsive Scale (NIMH-GOCS), the gold standards in terms of identifying OCD. In regards to Depression, your physician may turn to a survey known as PHQ-9 or even CIDI a more accurate yet still somewhat flawed assessment of depression. But all these surveys are considerably longer. They are not only much lengthier, but also more complex in terms of interpretation of the results. So, we will instead take our personal short, direct, although more general survey; just to see where we stand and if a more thorough screening tool is merited. Yes, for our purposes, they will do.

Obsessive Compulsive Survey (20)

*Fill in the circle of your choice.

Have you been bothered by unpleasant thoughts or images that repeatedly enter your mind, such as...?

1. concerns with contamination (dirt, germs, chemicals, radiation) or acquiring a serious illness such as AIDS?

   No   Yes

2. over concern with keeping objects (clothing, groceries, tools) in perfect order or arranged exactly?

   No   Yes

3. images of death or other horrible events?

   No   Yes

4. personally unacceptable religious or sexual thoughts?

   No   Yes

5. Have you worried a lot about terrible things happening, such as...fire, burglary, or flooding the house?

   No   Yes

6. accidentally hitting a pedestrian with your car, or letting your call roll down the hill?

No   Yes

7. spreading an illness or contracting one (such as the flu)?

No   Yes

8. losing something valuable?

No   Yes

9. harm coming to a loved one because you weren't careful enough?

No   Yes

10. Have you worried about acting on an unwanted and senseless urge or impulse, such as physically harming a loved one, pushing a stranger in front of a bus, steering your car into oncoming traffic; inappropriate sexual contact; or poisoning dinner guests?

No   Yes

11. Have you felt driven to perform certain acts over and over again, such as...excessive or ritualized washing, cleaning, or grooming, checking light

switches, water faucets, the stove, door locks, or emergency brake?

No   Yes

12. Do you exhibit the following behaviors: counting?

No   Yes

13. arranging; evening-up behaviors (making sure socks are at same height)?

No   Yes

14. collecting useless objects, inspecting the garbage before it is thrown out, or inspecting items before you purchase them?

No   Yes

15. repeating routine actions (in/out of chair, going through doorway, re-lighting cigarette) a certain number of times or until it feels just right?

No   Yes

16. need to touch objects or people?

No   Yes

17. unnecessary re-reading or re-writing; re-opening envelopes before they are mailed?

No   Yes

18. examine your body for signs of illness?

No   Yes

19. avoiding colors ("red" means blood), numbers ("1 3"
    is unlucky), or names (those that start with "D"
    signify death) that are associated with dreaded
    events or unpleasant thoughts?

No   Yes

20. needing to "confess" or repeatedly asking for
    reassurance that you said or did something
    correctly?

No   Yes

SCORE ____ /20

*If your score is approaching 15, you definitely
demonstrate clearly defined obsessive compulsive
behavior.

Depression Survey (21)

*Please assign each answer points in the following manner.

A "Not at all" would be a 0, while "Nearly every day" would be a 3.

1. Little interest or pleasure in doing things

Not at all
Several days
More than half the days
Nearly every day

Score:

2. Feeling down, depressed, or hopeless

Not at all
Several days
More than half the days
Nearly every day

Score:

3. Trouble falling or staying asleep or sleeping too much

Not at all
Several days
More than half the days
Nearly every day

Score:

4. Feeling tired or having little energy

Not at all
Several days
More than half the days
Nearly every day

Score:

5. Poor appetite or overeating

Not at all
Several days
More than half the days
Nearly every day

Score:

6. Feeling bad about yourself - or that you are a
failure or have let yourself or your family down

Not at all
Several days
More than half the days
Nearly every day

Score:

7. Trouble concentrating on things, such as reading
the newspaper or watching television

Not at all
Several days
More than half the days
Nearly every day

Score:

8. Moving or speaking so slowly that other people
could have noticed

Not at all
Several days
More than half the days
Nearly every day

Score:

9. Or the opposite - being so fidgety or restless that
you have been moving around a lot more than usual

Not at all
Several days
More than half the days
Nearly every day

Score:

10. Thoughts that you would be better off dead, or
of hurting yourself

Not at all
Several days
More than half the days
Nearly every day

SCORE _____ /30

*If your score is approaching 25, you definitely
demonstrate clearly defined depression.
Please, no matter what your score, don't let these
results trouble you. They are not exact measures of
either condition. They simply provide a barometer
for the way you are feeling, a way to see if there are
any red flags.

Take them, but don't be afraid if you see a red flag.
If you are feeling poorly, the only way to determine
if there is any basis for ongoing consultation or
medication is to see a doctor. I hope we are clear on
this. Let the professionals make the call.

If you have any questions about these conditions or
the books that I've written or you just need
someone in your shoes to chat with, please contact
me at **CKSt.Cross@gmail.com**. I want to help you.
It is why I write.

Works Cited

(1) "Obsessive Compulsive Disorder." NIMH. National Institute of Mental Health, January 2016. https://www.nimh.nih.gov/health/topics/obsessive-compulsive-disorder-ocd/index.shtml, April 2, 2018.

(2) "Depression." NIMH. National Institute of Mental Health, January 2016. https://www.nimh.nih.gov/health/topics/depression/index.shtml, April 2, 2018.

(3) "Anxiety Disorders." NIMH. National Institute of Mental Health, January 2016. https://www.nimh.nih.gov/health/topics/anxiety-disorders/index.shtml, April 2, 2018.

(4) Hayward, Jeff. "10 Symptoms of Obsessive-Compulsive Disorder." Activebeat. May 2016. https://www.activebeat.co/your-health/7-symptoms-of-obsessive-compulsive-disorder/?utm_medium=cpc&utm_source=google&utm_campaign=AB_GGL_US_DESK-SearchMarketing&utm_content=g_c_226195023723&cus_widget=kwd-11470866&utm_term=ocd&cus_teaser=&gclid=CjOKCQjwqYfWBRDPARIsABjQRYxZPHZkLQJ9YiJmiETqON HpvAc-xbV1wmMMQW6UXt1GRAPxiPQ5NUEaAmAfEALw_wcB. April 8, 2018.

(5) Hayward, Jeff. "Uncovering 8 Signs of Perfectly Hidden Depression." Activebeat. June 2016. https://www.activebeat.co/your-health/uncovering-8-signs-of-perfectly-hidden-depression/. April 20, 2018.

(6) McGauran, Debbie. "Let's Talk About Depression." Activebeat. June 2016.

https://www.activebeat.co/your-
health/women/lets-talk-about-depression/. May 1,
2018.

(7) "What is OCD." International OCD Foundation.
IOCDF, January 2018. https://iocdf.org/about-ocd/.
April 23, 2018.

(8) "What Causes OCD?." International OCD Foundation.
IOCDF, January 2018. https://iocdf.org/about-ocd/.
April 23, 2018.

(9) "What Is Obsessive-Compulsive Disorder?."
American Psychiatric Association. APA, January 2018.
https://www.psychiatry.org/patients-
families/ocd/what-is-obsessive-compulsive-disorder.
April 30, 2018.

(10) Parekh, Ranna. "Help with Depression." American
Psychiatric Association. APA. January 2017.
https://www.psychiatry.org/patients-
families/depression. May 6, 2018.

(11) "Obsessive-Compulsive Disorder (OCD) –
Medications." WebMD. June 2016.
https://www.webmd.com/mental-
health/tc/obsessive-compulsive-disorder-ocd-
medications. May 8, 2018.

(12) Goldberg, Joseph. "Surprising Signs of Depression."
WebMD. May 2016.
https://www.webmd.com/depression/ss/slideshow-
surprising-signs. May 18, 2018.

(13) "Causes of OCD." Obsessive Compulsive Disorder.
Psychology Today, January 2018.
https://www.psychologytoday.com/us/basics/ocd/c
auses-ocd. May 21, 2018.

(14) "Symptoms of Depression and OCD." Depression &
OCD. Psychology Today. January 2018.
https://www.psychologytoday.com/us/basics/depre
ssion/symptoms-depression. May 29, 2018.

(15) "Obsessive-Compulsive Disorder (OCD) Symptoms,
Treatment, and Self-Help". Helpguide. January 2018.
https://www.helpguide.org/articles/anxiety/obssessi
ve-compulsive-disorder-ocd.htm#obsessions. June 1,
2018.

(16) "Diagnostic Criteria for OCD", About Obsessive
Compulsive Disorder, Westwood Institute for
Anxiety Disorders, 2014.

(17) "Obsessive-compulsive disorder (OCD)." Mayo
Clinic. September 2016.
https://www.mayoclinic.org/diseases-
conditions/obsessive-compulsive-
disorder/symptoms-causes/syc-20354432. July 4,
2018.

18) "Depression Symptoms and Warning Signs
Recognizing Depression and Getting the Help You
Need." Help guide. January 2018.
https://www.helpguide.org/articles/depression/dep
ression-symptoms-and-warning-signs.htm. June 1,
2018.

19) "Depression (major depressive disorder)." Mayo
Clinic. February 2018.
https://www.mayoclinic.org/diseases-
conditions/depression/symptoms-causes/syc-
20356007. June 4, 2018.

20) Psych Central, OCD Quiz, John M. Grohol,
https://psychcentral.com/quizzes/ocdquiz.htm,
2017

21) "Mental Health America", Depression Survey, Staff,
http://www.mental healthamerica.net, 2017.

22) "Here's What We Learned From 83,000 Brain Scans",
Technology Works, Daniel Amen,
https://www.technologynetworks.com/neuroscienc
e/videos/heres-what-we-learned-from-83000-brain-
scans-297185

Author Biography

Charles K. St. Cross Sr. is a 49-year-old, inspired author with a tremendous amount of advice to share about his conditions, which he has battled his whole life. He is a sufferer of acute Obsessive Compulsive Disorder and severe Depression. He grew up in southwest Connecticut in a household full of family who exhibited several symptoms of the aforementioned conditions.

He was a gifted child who grew up to be only the second family member to go to college. Charles holds three university degrees and has spent time in business and education. OCD and Depression knows no race, creed, color, or education and despite his academic prowess and varied professional experience, Charles still suffers. He is married with two sons. The small happiness's he finds are with his dear family and with the opportunity to help others through his writing. It was his esteemed psychiatrist who suggested he use his vast knowledge of his conditions and numerous treatment experiences to relate to others who endure the same or similar conditions.

Charles took this as a great and special compliment and began pouring his life into the book you hold in your hands. It is his greatest hope that it will support people in need of advice or just someone with whom to relate. Charles assures that helping even one person would be enough.

His goals are two. Humbly, he simply hopes his almost five decades of suffering were not in vain, and someone out there can gain just a little happiness from his words. In addition, his supreme hope is that his writing will change the life of someone battling the same demons he has faced himself. He speaks from his head and his heart. He is honored for you to listen.

www.ingramcontent.com/pod-product-compliance
Lightning Source LLC
Chambersburg PA
CBHW072243260726
48657CB00001BA/426